63215

3 2222 0068 081

MW00738000

5

Praise for *Building the Team Organization*

"Dean Tjosvold has been a major contributor to the understanding of teams and organizations through his original, important theoretical and research publications. In this well-written book, he and Mary Tjosvold provide a brilliant and practical discussion of everything one would want to know about teams whether you are a social scientist, a practitioner, or simply a curious reader."

—Morton Deutsch, E.L. Thorndike Professor Emeritus of Psychology; Director Emeritus of the Morton Deutsch International Center for Cooperation and Conflict Resolution (MD-ICCCR) Teachers College, Columbia University

"Finally, we have two scholars who offer us the critical perspective and management insights in developing an adaptive team organization that can lead us the way in collaborating with the ever-evolving stakeholders of the 21st century, and in meeting the ever-pressing challenge of a teamwork economy in the foreseeable future."

—Michael Y. K. Chan, Chairman, Cafe de Coral Group; Chairman, Business Enterprise Management Center, Hong Kong Management Association

"The truth is that you can't expect to achieve extraordinary results all by yourself. Cooperative goals and open-minded discussions are what Dean and Mary help us understand is what it takes to lead and be part of an extraordinary team, backed up by solid research, their own and from other scholars, located in both the West and East, providing key universal insights and many very practical applications. Full of insightful and pragmatic do's and don'ts!"

—Barry Z. Posner, PhD, Accolti Endowed Professor of Leadership, Dean (1997–2009) Leavey School of Business, Santa Clara University; co-author, *The Leadership Challenge* and *Making Extraordinary Things Happen in Asia*

"A perfect blend of seasoned academic wisdom and proactive hands-on management and leadership experience. The authors have themselves set a great example of a productive team by building a highly inspiring product – an elegant model of teamwork to be adopted by enthusiastic team builders all over the world. A well-formulated global model of teamwork which can be applied in many group, intergroup, and organizational settings. The authors have successfully used the power of 'docudrama' with plausible characters and lively dialogues resonating with human concerns and constructive humor."

—Hasan Saraç, Business Consultant & Author or Management Consultant & Author, Turkey

"*Building the Team Organization* is full of great advice for making teamwork in organizations productive by emphasizing cooperative goals and open discussion. And importantly, all that advice is grounded in sound research, making the book a resource for both students and managers."
— Jeanne M. Brett, DeWitt W. Buchanan, Jr. Professor of Dispute Resolution and Negotiations, Kellogg School of Management, Northwestern University

"The book postulates that teams run an organization, not individuals. Positive team dynamics are crucial to any successful organization. The book aptly identifies various potentially destructive team conflicts and proposes pragmatic models to turning them into constructive contributions. While easy to read, the book also provides convenient lists of do's and don'ts where appropriate."
— Peter Lau, Chairman and CEO, Giordano International Limited

"Dean and Mary Tjosvold have written a remarkable book on how to build a team organization. I especially like the breadth and depth of the book and their willingness to address the most complex and difficult issues in team and organizational building. It is a book that both students and professionals will continue to use for years to come. The book, utilizing interesting case studies, takes the reader through the process of building effective teams that cooperate with each other in maximizing overall organizational effectiveness. While covering the theory and research underlying team and organizational effectiveness in clear and easily understood ways, the Tjosvolds give helpful, practical advice on how to implement the knowledge into action. A 'must-have' book for anyone interested in team and organizational effectiveness."
— David W. Johnson, Emeritus Professor, Educational Psychology, University of Minnesota; Co-Director of the Cooperative Learning Center; Emma M. Birkmaier Professorship in Educational Leadership at the University of Minnesota (1994–1997) and the Libra Endowed Chair for Visiting Professor at the University of Maine (1996–1997)

"This book is a blueprint for organizations striving to become more productive, humane, and ethical. Easy-reading, based on modern management principles, and with real-life examples it will create work places of dignity, meaning, and community for a global society."
— Wayne Jennings, PhD, Leader of the chartered alternative school movement, St Paul, MN

Building the Team Organization

How to Open Minds, Resolve Conflict, and Ensure Cooperation

Dean Tjosvold
*Henry Y. W. Fong Chair Professor of Management,
Lingnan University, Hong Kong*

Mary Tjosvold
CEO, Mary T. Inc, USA

First published 2015 by
PALGRAVE MACMILLAN

Palgrave Macmillan in the UK is an imprint of Macmillan Publishers Limited, registered in England, company number 785998, of Houndmills, Basingstoke, Hampshire RG21 6XS.

Palgrave Macmillan in the US is a division of St Martin's Press LLC, 175 Fifth Avenue, New York, NY10010.

Palgrave Macmillan is the global academic imprint of the above companies and has companies and representatives throughout the world.

Palgrave® and Macmillan® are registered trademarks in the United States, the United Kingdom, Europe and other countries.

ISBN 978–0–230–24712–3

This book is printed on paper suitable for recycling and made from fully managed and sustained forest sources. Logging, pulping and manufacturing processes are expected to conform to the environmental regulations of the country of origin.

A catalogue record for this book is available from the British Library.

A catalog record for this book is available from the Library of Congress.

Typeset by MPS Limited, Chennai, India.

To Margaret and Dale

Table of Contents

Preface

Building a Team Organization will help you and your teammates learn to work as a team. You can study our model of productive teamwork together to develop a common understanding of the kind of team you want to become. You can use this understanding along with the book's procedures and examples to develop methods and approaches so that you and your team members succeed.

Teams may seem like a new idea that contemporary organizations have recently discovered and now are harnessing to complete many vital tasks from hiring chief executive officers (CEOs) to building 25-mile-long bridges. But teams are our oldest, most adaptive social innovation. Our ancestors came to understand that they could not only survive but flourish in family and community groups. Later they realized that getting teams to work with each other within organizations could be even more powerful. We still use organizations to wage war and to make peace; we work, pray, celebrate, and play in groups and organizations.

We have good reasons for relying on teams and organizations. Productive teamwork enhances individuals as well as accomplishes important tasks. However, teamwork is a "more for more" solution. Teamwork gives a lot but it also requires a lot.

Leaders and team members often argue that developing teamwork is so difficult because of motivation; people just do not want to work as a team. They blame people's inherent egotism and selfishness. We hear about people who are "free riders" who care only about themselves in our classrooms, workshops, and family business; indeed sometimes we meet these people.

It's more often, though, that people want to work as a team but fail to do so despite their motivation. We all have had friends, family, clubs, sports, work, religious and community groups, and organizations that we consider warmly and believe they make our lives meaningful. However, working productively as a team takes much more than just wanting to.

Getting people, especially when they are from different departments, organizations, and cultures with different specialties, to work together effectively is challenging. An individual cannot work with others by him or herself. Each member, as well as the leader, needs to decide to work as a team. Developing teamwork is something people do together.

The Productive Teamwork Model

We all receive advice about how we can live and work productively with other people. Everyone has his or her own theories of the nature of quality relationships and the best ways to work and live with others. Some people, for example, think a decisive leader is necessary; others believe that leadership must be shared.

Researchers too have many ways to characterize effective teams; indeed, there are many ingredients that contribute to teamwork. But a concise, documented model can be a very useful guide so that managers and team members have a common understanding of the kind of team they are working to become. Then they can develop common plans for the relationships and ways of working that are useful for them.

Hundreds of studies have documented that this book's model of teamwork applies in many group, intergroup, and organizational settings, including between organizations, in Asia as well as the West. The book's reference section identifies key studies and reviews of the research supporting this model. Readers can find more detailed treatment of the research in these publications.

Team members, leaders and employees, top management team members, supply chain partners, competitors, business managers, and government officials have been found to be more effective when they believe their goals are cooperative and express their diverse opinions and integrate their ideas open-mindedly. This teamwork has helped them innovate, reduce costs, reflect upon and learn from their experience, and strengthen their confidence and relationships.

The particular methods and procedures to work as a team, though, depend upon the situation. For some teams, ten-minute meetings at the beginning and end of the workday are very useful; for others, the most effective method is to meet every month for an afternoon. Effective teams have many different procedures and methods. However, our model of relationships and interaction has been found to characterize effective teams in many situations.

Building a Team Organization's model has two fundamental components: Cooperative goals and open-minded discussion. With cooperative goals, people understand that they are better off by helping each other succeed than by pursuing their own goals at the expense of others. Open-minded discussion asks team members to express their ideas but also to put themselves in each other's shoes to understand and integrate their ideas. Chapter 1 elaborates on the model and its research. The remaining chapters discuss and illustrate how your team can apply this model to your situation.

The cooperative goals and open-minded discussion framework is elegant but it is not simple or easy to do. Leaders and members must learn and appreciate these ideas, develop ways to apply them in their own setting, and work continually to reflect upon their experiences and improve their teamwork. Developing cooperative, open-minded teamwork is an ongoing journey, not a one or two-step procedure.

We have developed this book to help you and your colleagues understand and apply the teamwork model to make your teams more productive and enhancing. Like most achievements, this book is a product of teamwork. Dean has conducted research on teamwork since 1970; Mary has practiced teamwork as a teacher, done research on education and management, and has led our family business even longer. (Mary is the older sister!) Together we have developed a research-based, practical book that neither of us could have done alone.

The Story of One Team

Every team member is unique; working with one person is not like working with another person. If an accountant leaves your team, the next accountant will not be the same as the one who left. Each team is unique. Its ways have to fit its members, situation, and tasks.

Readings, though, can make teamwork seem abstract, even portraying a well-functioning team as a machine that just needs the correct "inputs." In addition to a few cases of organizations developing teamwork, we have developed a story so that you can see managers and employees applying the teamwork model over time in ways that fits them and their challenges. The story of Community Bank is based on actual examples from teams and organizations we know but it should be considered a docudrama, not a report of actual events. The story shows how the teamwork model can be introduced and used to strengthen teams, organizations, and their partnerships.

Our Aspirations

Our book has three sections. Section I, Productive Teamwork, describes and examines the teamwork model and identifies concrete ways to apply the model. Section II, Building Team Relationships, examines and shows through a docudrama how to strengthen leadership, develop cooperative goals, foster open-minded discussion, and manage conflict. Section III, Making the Organization a Team, focuses on teamwork within and between organizations, that is, working with customers, forming cross functional groups, and developing productive partnerships with other organizations. It discusses how we can build vibrant, diverse communities. The book concludes with ideas and practices to reflect upon and to continue to strengthen teamwork.

Building a Team Organization describes the fundamental nature of productive teamwork but recognizes that teams must develop their own ways of working. It helps you and your teammates forge a common understanding of what makes relationships and working together constructive, and shows you how you can together use your common understanding to develop methods of working effectively for your team and situation.

We hope you use our book to make your teams stronger, more meaningful, and more productive. Then you and we will succeed together.

Acknowledgments

A larger team very much supports the author team. Our parents, Dale and Margaret, were our leaders to have rich, loving cooperative experiences growing up together along with our older brother, Dale. Mary always had Dean's back, even when that meant losing her Street Patrol duty for aggressively reminding our older neighbor, Albert, he was not to hit her young brother. We have many happy memories and feel fortunate to have such a great family.

Later Margaret translated her considerable abilities to begin and develop our family business of providing residential services for people with special needs. Margaret continues to support and inspire our clients, employees, and partners. We have learned a lot watching her up-close.

Margaret also inspires the next generation, Jason, Wesley, Lena, and Colleen. We know they are well prepared to lead good, full lives and to contribute to others both outside and inside the company.

We also want to thank the people at Palgrave Macmillan for their support in developing and publishing the book. Many colleagues and friends have helped and encouraged us. David W. Johnson has ably and warmly supported our learning about teams and cooperation and competition for decades. Bill Swanson, who is like the third son in the family, gave us wise advice. Readers can thank him for a shorter book.

Productive Teamwork

From the standpoint of everyday life ... there is one thing we do know; that man is here for the sake of other men— above all, for those upon whose smile and well-being our own happiness depends, and also for the countless unknown souls with whose fate we are connected by a bond of sym- pathy. Many times a day I realize how much of my own outer and inner life is built upon the labours of my fellow men, both living and dead, and how earnestly I must exert myself in order to give in return as much as I have received.

Albert Einstein

chapter 1

Teambuilding is Necessary

I am of the opinion that my life belongs to the whole community, and as long as I live, it is my privilege to do for it whatever I can.

George Bernard Shaw

Vineet Nayar (2010) was convinced that HCL Technologies, an information technology (IT) services provider based in Delhi, had to change if it was to meet the demands of customers for long-term partners, not just to hire discrete IT services. HCL did change. From 2005 to 2009, and despite the financial crisis of 2008, it nearly tripled its annual revenue, doubled its market capitalization, and was acclaimed as a best employer in India. Perhaps most significantly, it had developed an Employees First, Customers Second (EFCS) culture.

Nayar had the insight that he could not just transform his company single-handedly. He could not just take the "leap" into a new organization culture by himself; he had to help everyone take the "leap." For people to work for change, they had to be convinced themselves that the present ways of operating were inadequate and that there was a clearly superior, viable alternative.

But how can thousands of employees become convinced that change is needed and possible? Nayar realized that giving charismatic speeches, even if he could, was insufficient; active participation was necessary. He met senior managers in small groups and employees in large meetings to challenge them to face the reality of HCL's current position. These gatherings as well as meetings with customers helped to develop the alternative where the emphasis would be on customers partnering with HCL employees to provide IT solutions, which grew into the EFCS culture. Later these gatherings came to be called Mirror Mirror and were relied upon to reflect on HCL and plan for change.

In 2005, Nayar invited 100 senior managers for three days to form a strategy to define and implement the EFCS culture. Rather than talk and persuade, Nayar encouraged discussion where managers voiced their ideas and hopes but also their concerns, their "Yes, buts…". Some managers feared that HCL would fail to win global customers while losing its local base; other managers raised questions about specific strategies; still others wanted to charge ahead quickly. Three days of expressing their views fully, listening to each other, and refining their strategies helped to build a solid consensus.

Employees also needed to appreciate the need for change and to understand the EFCS culture. Nayar held company-wide meetings called Directions that, though they might include 4,000 employees, stimulated discussion and thinking. To set an open atmosphere, Nayar began by dancing around the room to Bollywood music, asking individual employees to dance with him. He reasoned that employees would then see him as an open-minded person, though not a particularly good dancer, and be willing to voice their concerns. Indeed, two hours of animated discussion typically followed his opening remarks.

Small-scale catalysts complemented discussions on culture. An on-line system facilitated employees making suggestions and lodging complaints; staff recorded whether their manager's response was satisfactory. This program put managers in the service of front-line employees, making the EFCS culture concrete.

HCL had a 360-degree feedback program to reinforce the need for managers and others to work together up and down and across the hierarchy. But few people gave their manager feedback. Nayar put his results on-line for everyone in the company to see and to give people more incentive to provide feedback to him. Many managers followed suit, revitalizing the 360-degree feedback program.

Managers and employees were given access to financial data on the company as a whole to appreciate the need for change and to measure their progress. Rather than review each of his 100 managers' business plans himself, Nayar asked them to place videos on the company intranet where managers reviewed and discussed each other's plans.

Employee First Councils reinforced that HCL valued individual employees and helped them to pursue their interests and values outside work. Employees formed groups around specific "passions" from art and music, to philanthropy and social responsibility. These councils helped to integrate work and personal lives, making work more meaningful.

Nayar also developed a good working relationship with the board. The board wanted to discuss major decisions before they were made and Nayar wanted their experience and support. The best way was to work transparently where Nayar kept them informed with frequent reports and meetings.

A Team Organization Leader

Vineet Nayar was a leader. He understood that the essence of leadership is working with and through others where others are not just direct reports. That meant that at HCL he should work with and through the thousands of employees worldwide as well as his own board. He listened to customers but he recognized that his primary focus should be to strengthen and prepare employees—"Employees First"—who then could take care of customers—"Customers Second."

He was a team leader. Recognizing the value of teamwork, he developed various platforms and settings that encouraged managers and employees to work together. He vitalized the 360-degree feedback to let other leaders know that they worked with and through many people. Rather than provide feedback to managers individually, he had them share their plans with each other so that they could comment and brainstorm together. Rather than announce decisions, he and managers hammered out the company's strategic plans together.

Specifically, Nayar was a team builder; he realized that it is not enough to put people in one room and call them a team. He could set the stage but he recognized that individuals must make these teams work; they must choose to commit to making their teams succeed. Before they will "leap" they must themselves be convinced that the teams are valuable to the company as well as useful for themselves. Despite the size of HCL, he encouraged everyone to consider the company's strategies and methods; he worked for a shared understanding of the issues and difficulties and common solutions to deal with them.

To encourage open-minded teamwork, he kept his own speeches short, listened more than persuaded, and even danced to show that he was open and not afraid of showing his limitations. He realized that people must share their reservations as well as their enthusiasm; otherwise they may well build up their doubts about the value and the methods that Nayar was proposing. "Yes, buts," if unanswered, harden into resistance to change.

Team Building's Contributions

Vineet Nayar and HCL illustrate central points about building a team organization. Teamwork is valuable, indeed, needed for organizations, employees, and their customers; but it must be nurtured and developed. Leaders can play a critical role by laying the groundwork and setting directions, but managers and employees must take up the challenge and make their teams work. Team members must express their ideas and frustrations, listen and understand, and combine their ideas to solve problems. They must channel their energies and work out their frustrations with each other. Nayar, or indeed any other leader, cannot do that alone.

Nayar and the managers and employees at HCL had good reasons to develop and make their teams work. They were investing in teamwork to strengthen themselves so that, in turn, they could serve their customers. Then they could develop HCL into a company in which they would build their career and develop their lives.

Teambuilding is rational. HCL employees had to "leap"—they had to commit themselves to the company and to building it as a team organization. Emotions propel this leaping and the leap stimulates a great many feelings. However, the leap is rational as well as emotional. Nayar did not expect employees to leap blindly and follow him; they had to understand that this new team organization would pay off for themselves and their customers.

Teamwork is highly valuable and well worth investment because it serves essential conditions for effective organizations. Teamwork helps organizations to serve their customers; no organization can survive without the support and sponsorship of the people it serves. The second central condition is that an organization requires the energy and commitment of its people; teamwork can help employees find their organizational work valuable, as it helps them meet core needs and reach aspirations.

Organizations must serve customers and employees when marketplaces and, indeed, societies are changing. As illustrated by HCL, teamwork helps organizations manage change so that they can revitalize themselves as they adapt and take advantage of the evolving marketplace and world in order to serve their customers and their employees.

The next section briefly reviews knowledge, showing that teams have major advantages when it comes to innovation within organizations and provide more value to their customers. Considerable research has also demonstrated that teamwork is good for individuals as well as the organization as a whole. Teamwork is essential to adapt to the changing environment.

Teamwork to Serve Customers

Cooperative, open-minded teamwork is key to providing value to customers. Research has shown that these teams can overcome obstacles and innovate to develop new products and services that serve customers' needs. Teamwork is also needed to solve important customer complaints and problems. In relationship marketing, employees and customers become their own team, committed to meeting customer goals and thereby creating customer loyalty to the company.

Innovation

Companies innovate by creating new, valued products and services, but also by developing new technology and methods that help them deliver their products and services more effectively to their customers. Innovation in an organization, though, is much more than a bright insight or a quick flash of inspiration. Teamwork where employees and managers work together is needed to confront and overcome significant hurdles and take the many steps needed to innovate in organizations.

Innovators must find problems and situations and turn them into opportunities. They cannot just throw up their hands in frustration, but need to use this frustration to dig deeper into the situation and think of alternatives.

Once the issue is understood, people must create different solutions. Typically, modifications of old approaches are first discussed but found unsatisfactory. Feeling blocked and frustrated, people may feel pessimistic and withdraw. During this period of frustration and doubt, ideas incubate as the problem is considered from several perspectives. Sometimes the solution comes in a great illumination: The "Aha! I've got it!" experience. Then the solution is elaborated and selected for more careful testing.

Creative solutions by their very nature can be highly damaging and costly. They must be vigorously tested and evaluated. Prototypes, field tests, demonstration projects, focus groups, and surveys are used to collect data. People debate and challenge each other's conclusions and implications drawn from the data.

Well-tested ideas and insights are necessary for innovation in organizations, but so is persistence. People must be motivated to make the effort and bear the frustration and tension that usually accompany innovation and change. They need to believe that they have the courage and imagination and find working on innovations rewarding and exciting.

Innovators must overcome resistance. People are often comfortable with the status quo, have been rewarded for reliable, stable performance, and will want good reasons for why they should go through the effort required to make changes. They may suspect that the innovation will work against their interests, power, and status. They want to be convinced that the innovation is cost-effective, fair, has acceptable risks, does not stretch resources too far, and promotes long-term interests.

Individuals working alone cannot be expected to overcome all these hurdles and innovate. Effective teamwork throughout the organization is necessary.

Solve Customer Problems

Contemporary managers recognize that they must stay in touch and listen to their customers. Not only are retail stores and other consumer companies taking their customers more seriously, professional organizations, governmental agencies, and regulated companies are too. They must listen to customers who are frustrated with their service. But listening is only a first step. Companies must also respond to customer complaints and concerns. Successful companies listen open-mindedly, act appropriately, and use customer problems to improve service and win more customers. Teamwork is necessary to develop high quality customer service.

Serving customers is not accomplished by the skill and flair of individual salespersons. Coordinated action is needed to respond to customer problems successfully. Not often can the employee who hears the complaint solve the problem alone. The employee who listens must communicate and get others to assist in solving the problem. Especially in larger, bureaucratic companies, employees from different departments and outlooks have to coordinate. To market high technology effectively, for example, service, training, engineers, and technical personnel must coordinate with each other and with salespersons (Tjosvold, Meredith, and Wong, 1998).

As we have seen, HCL was learning that their customers wanted solutions to their problems, not simply technical expertise. It is not enough to give a client various kinds of computer knowledge or a solution that makes sense from only one standpoint. Clients want a solution that integrates the knowledge bases into a coherent approach that will work for them. To win and fulfill contracts, engineers and technology specialists must bring their various expertise and experience to bear and find ways to incorporate them. Nayar and other managers were working to develop a culture and vision, compensation system, and evaluation procedures that encourage and reward teamwork across functional areas among various specialists to serve customers.

Teamwork to Enhance Employees

Organizations must serve their customers to survive and prosper; but for innovation to happen and customer relationships to be developed, employees must make intense commitments. They must take the long-term view, suffer through frustrations, and master hurdles to help their companies adapt, often with little immediate recognition or reward. Organizations need employees to be good citizens. Not all desired and important behavior is prescribed in job descriptions or stipulated in union contracts. Staying late to deal with a crisis, assisting an overloaded colleague, and listening to a distressed employee all contribute to a successful organization. Employees must care about the company and each other. In HCL terms, employees are first.

Being part of a team is potentially a very rich and rewarding experience for individuals. Through them, people can meet the human need to achieve, be part of a larger effort, and feel accepted. Increasingly people are forming voluntary self-help groups to cope with cancer, divorce, abuse, and death.

Human beings are now called social animals and indeed they may be the most social animal. Working together is part of our human heritage; we are built for groups. Indeed, Homo sapiens were not stronger or faster than other animals, but were able to join forces for hunting and protection. They needed to coordinate their activities and this need stimulated language and intellectual development. Parents' emotional bonds and care allow children to develop their abilities over many years. Humans' social nature very much contributed to our emerging as the dominating species. Though we live very differently than our ancestors, our underlying needs are similar.

Need Fulfillment

Psychologists have developed various frameworks to understand human needs, motives, and instincts. There is general agreement that needs to achieve, affiliate, and have power play an important role in our behavior (McClelland, 1987). People want to achieve; they want to complete tasks at a standard of excellence. They like challenging but attainable tasks, because they feel an internal sense of accomplishment and realize that it was possible for them to fail. People try to meet achievement needs in a great many ways: Building a bridge, climbing a mountain, getting an "A" on a report card, creating a company, planting a garden, or developing and marketing a new product.

Affiliation involves the desire to associate and feel recognized and accepted by others. People want to be noticed and valued. They will seek the assurance and company of others, especially when feeling stressed and anxious. These affiliation needs are particularly strong with significant others, but even the regard of strangers can be important. People have a great many ways of meeting these needs: Some demand, some ask, some give in order to get, and others hope.

People also have needs for power; they want to have an impact on others and to influence them. It propels some individuals to try to dominate and control; some fantasize about great power and recognition; others want give-and-take collaboration where they are influenced as well as influence.

Researchers have shown that people differ in the strength of achievement, affiliation, and power needs and their abilities and ways to meet them. However, the more fundamental finding is that everyone has them. Unfortunately, some people have developed unacceptable ways to meet them (e.g., bank robbers, drug lords); other people, demoralized through years of frustration, try to suppress their social needs rather than meet them.

Productive teams are vital ways for individuals to meet their achievement, affiliation, and power needs. Team members feel internal pride and accomplishment as their team completes challenging tasks that they could not accomplish alone. They feel part of a larger effort and accepted as valuable colleagues in their mutual work. Through the give and take of team effort, they meet their needs to influence and have an impact on others.

R E W A R D I N G   W O R K

Surveys suggest that employees want traditional economic benefits of job security, opportunities to make as much money as they can, and good retirement programs. But they want more: Their work should be valuable itself (Kasser and Ryan, 1993). In a survey, 88 per cent of US employees said it was personally important to them to work hard and to do their best on the job. In another survey, the majority of respondents agreed with the statement that they have an inner need to do the very best job they can, regardless of pay. Only one out of four thought a job was an economic necessity or simply an economic transaction. Employees want their companies to succeed in order to give them well-paying jobs and make their work meaningful and rewarding.

Social Support

Feeling connected to other people, having meaningful relationships, being able to rely on others, having other people to turn to for assistance, and feeling satisfied with one's friends all provide social support (Bolger and Eckenrode, 1991). This support helps people to be productive and achieve, avoid distressing feelings of isolation, live longer lives, recover from illness and injury faster, and experience less threatening illnesses.

Isolation runs counter to our nature. Loneliness is one of the most painful human experiences. Feeling estranged undermines psychological wellbeing and the quality of life; it even shortens life itself. Sadly, surveys indicate that depression is growing rapidly in the United States; there has been a tenfold increase in the rate of depression in the last two generations (Seligman, 1988; Shenk, 2009). It is likely that breakdowns of relationships in families and communities have created unprecedented feelings of loneliness, hopelessness, and self-rejection.

A great deal of research indicates that social support provides the care and information necessary to cope with stress, maintain a sense of wellbeing and self-esteem, and flourish physically and psychologically (Kirmeyer and Lin, 1987). Forming links with organizational superiors and more experienced peers through formal and informal mentoring programs can help new employees adjust to the organization (Tjosvold, Meredith, and Wong, 1998). Feelings of being cared for and emotionally valued encourage conscientious work, willingness to be good citizens, and contributions to innovations (Eisenberger, Fasolo, and Davis-LaMastro, 1990).

Feeling connected with supportive others provides opportunities to demonstrate one's own compassion and capability by helping others (Jecker and Landy, 1969). As Leo Tolstoy, the novelist, wrote: "We do not love people so much for the good they have done us, as for the good we have done them." Helping others induces a sense of responsibility and involvement with others.

People also depend upon others to understand and come to terms with reality. They want to be correct in their analysis of their social world.

Wanting some assurance that they are experiencing the world in a sensible, sane manner, people turn to others for comparison.

Self-Esteem

Self-esteem of judging oneself as a worthwhile person very much affects wellbeing and competence. People who value themselves, for example, make more favorable impressions on job recruiters and get more job offers; they also more effectively cope with job loss. Low self-esteem leads to emotional problems, poor achievement, awkward social relations, susceptibility to influence, and rejection of others (Brockner, 1988).

Personal attitudes about oneself are grounded in relationships. People develop their own sense of self and self-esteem by considering how others see and treat them (Mead, 1934). They see themselves through the mirror of other's eyes; if others tell them they are outgoing, people tend to see themselves as outgoing. Our innermost thoughts about ourselves depend upon others. To the extent others value us, we value ourselves.

Teams are powerful drivers of individual enhancement. Through teams, people can feel fulfilled by superior achievement, see themselves as part of a larger effort, feel supported, and strengthen their self-esteem. Teams can very much serve employees as well as customers.

Teamwork to Manage Change

Organizations must not only serve customers and employees, now they have to continue to do so under rapidly changing conditions. HCL illustrates that teamwork is needed to develop and build an organization so that it can respond to changes and provide more value to customers. Vineet Nayar recognized that he alone, even with inspiring speeches, could not get HCL employees to leap into the EFCS culture. Yet leaping is not enough, the culture has to be constructed and developed; employees can develop this culture by working together in their Mirror Mirror, Directions, 360-degree feedback, and other settings. Employees and managers had to extend their culture and develop ways, habits, and procedures to express and make use of their culture.

Nayar and his team of thousands managed change and repositioned HCL to serve customers effectively. They began by forming various sessions to discuss issues together and develop strategies and specific plans to strengthen themselves. They used various team sessions to build their team organization focused on customers.

They had ideas about the nature of the teamwork they wanted to develop. Their aim was not just to have teams and joint sessions but also to make use of these opportunities to work together productively. They realized that it was not simply getting together; they had to create the open culture that would help people speak their minds, but also listen to each other and combine their ideas into common solutions. Nayar was willing to dance with employees in the hopes of developing openness as a value to guide their teamwork.

Conclusions

Teams can be powerful drivers of organizational success. This chapter has reviewed the considerable research documenting the potential value of teams for companies and individuals. However, teams must be well structured and managed if they are going to serve customers and employees and continue to do so as society and markets change. Fortunately, we can draw upon a great deal of research to understand the nature of productive teamwork. Chapter 2 presents our model of the key ingredients to productive teamwork and begins to show how managers and employees can use the model to strengthen their teamwork.

Action Plans

Do less of:

- Expect teamwork to happen automatically.
- Try to impose teamwork.
- Assume teamwork promotes either the organization or employees.
- Support customers but not employees.

Do more of:

- Appreciate that problems are solved and things get done through relationships.
- Encourage the whole organization to appreciate the value of teamwork.
- Teamwork serves customers as it stimulates innovative products and responds to their concerns.
- Teamwork enhances employees as it facilitates social support and heightens self-confidence.
- Individuals meet needs for achievement, affiliation, and social power in teams.
- Teamwork helps organizations manage change.
- Recognize that teamwork is rational as its benefits are more than its costs.

chapter 2

What Makes Teams Effective?

In a large business, the most important determinant of success is the effectiveness of millions of day-to-day interactions between human beings. If those contacts are contentious, turf-oriented, and parochial, the company will flounder, bureaucracies will grow, and internal competition will be rampant. But when employees behave in accountable, team-oriented and collegial ways, it dramatically improves group effectiveness.

Raymond Smith, CEO, Bell Atlantic (Kanter, 1991).

Vineet Nayar wanted his team of thousands to leap with him to manage change and reposition HCL to serve customers more effectively. Realizing that he could not impose his will on his staff, he organized sessions where together they developed the organization's culture and strategies. But to make these sessions effective, he wanted to create an open culture that would help managers and employees speak their minds as well as listen to each other and combine their ideas into common solutions to move forward.

Nayar understood that it was effective, open-minded teamwork that would help them to manage change, serve customers effectively, and enhance people. His aim was not just to have team sessions but also to make use of these opportunities to discuss issues directly and develop common solutions.

Nayar also realized that he had to give his employees an understanding about how they should discuss with each other and work together to achieve their goals. He had ideas about what he could do to communicate that they needed open-minded teamwork. As we mentioned in Chapter 1, Nayar would not only meet with his employees, he would dance with them. This dancing, he anticipated, would powerfully communicate that he was an approachable boss, that they really were partners, and that they might break some rules and have fun together as they created a new HCL.

Employees have their own ideas about what makes teamwork effective; everyday they draw on and test their ideas about the best ways to work with others. Nayar worked and danced to emphasize certain ideas that he thought would help them to work effectively together. He realized that HCL managers and employees had to understand and be committed to work as an open-minded team. All managers and employees are needed to make their HCL team effective. A shared understanding of what makes a team effective clarifies their common goal.

ESPOUSING AND USING THEORIES

Chris Argyris (1976) argued that we develop ideas about how we should live and work with others. We have a wide variety of "when in this situation, do this" rules: He called this implicit knowledge theories-in-use. We also have espoused theories of how we think we should work with colleagues—which often contradict theories-in-use; managers talk one-way, act another. For example, most managers advocate that employees should participate in making decisions so that they become committed to implementing them. However, the actions of many managers reveal that they actually want to impose their own solutions. Discrepancies between the ideas people espouse and actions they take add confusion and further complicate developing teamwork.

Need for a Model of Productive Teamwork

Team members may all be committed to making their team productive and enhancing for all but have different understandings of what makes teamwork effective. They can end up working at cross-purposes despite their intentions.

Confusions about Teamwork

Misunderstandings about what makes a team productive often lead to considerable frustration. For some people, effective team members keep their differences quiet so as not to embarrass each other and disrupt the smoothness and efficiency of their joint work. They are upset with team members who express their opposing ideas and identify their frustrations; they see these people as immature, self-interested, and uninterested in working as a team.

In contrast, team members who believe in open conflict are annoyed with those who avoid it as they fail to speak their minds. It seems to them that their teammates would rather have the team make mistakes and ignore issues than make their team work.

When people have difficulty working together, they tend to blame others for not being motivated. "My team members do not care; they are social loafers. They are just self-interested; they just want to do it their own way. No one can work with these people." A few individuals may not want to work as a team, but confusions about teamwork and poor team skills are much more significant obstacles than motivation.

A Good Theory of Teamwork

Kurt Lewin, the founder of contemporary social psychology, argued: "There is *nothing so practical as a good theory.*" Theoretical understanding of teamwork contributes very substantially to its practice.

What makes a theory practical? A good theory of teamwork identifies the characteristics that very much impact team effectiveness. We need grandiose theories that make powerful predictions rather than picayune theories of subtle effects (Deutsch, 1973; Schmidt, 2010). We should understand the "underlying simplicity" of social relationships rather than their "superficial complexity."

We want to know the characteristics that contribute substantially to making teams productive and enhancing. A practical theory of teamwork identifies the relationships and interactions that help employees and managers make their teams productive.

WHEN DO TEAMMATES ENGAGE IN SOCIAL LOAFING AND FREE RIDING?

Social loafing occurs when people exert less effort working in a group than when they work alone (Karau and Williams, 1993; Latané, Williams, and Harkins, 1979). Many students and employees worry that teammates will engage in free riding because others will make up for their lack of effort. They seem far less worried about their own social loafing!

Studies document that individuals in teams can work less than when they are alone, but also suggest the conditions in which social loafing does and does not occur. Social loafing is far from inevitable; considerable research shows that individuals can and often work hard in groups.

In social loafing studies, individuals were found to exert less effort when shouting and clapping in a group than when alone (Latané et al., 1979). Individuals did not have their own task to do for the group but merely shouted and clapped together. Shouting and clapping are not very meaningful or interesting tasks in themselves. The people in the group knew that their fellow team members could not monitor their performance nor know whether they worked hard or not. The task was completed in one setting; teammates had no prior or future relationship with each other. These conditions can occur in groups but are atypical. Perhaps most significantly, individuals in organizations nearly always have ongoing relationships with each other. Teammates typically know each other, monitor each other's efforts, and express their appreciation or disapproval for each other's performance. Individuals realize that their teammates might hold them accountable for their effort or lack of effort. Failure to work on group tasks risks complicating and undermining their relationships. The social environment, especially the relationships among people, has very significant effects on individuals, including their social loafing.

Studies when taken together suggest that individuals work harder and more effectively in groups than individuals working alone in most organizational settings (Johnson and Johnson, 2005; Johnson, Johnson, and Tjosvold, 2014). However, individuals should develop cooperative relationships and open-minded discussions to be so motivated and productive. Results show that individuals with competitive or independent goals are not highly motivated or productive. Groups must be well structured and managed in order to yield constructive effects.

Ongoing relationships do not themselves ensure that there will be no social loafing or free riders. When team members develop competitive and independent relationships with each other, they may be so frustrated that they work hard to social loaf and be free riders. They want to reciprocate and frustrate their team members and one way to do that is to do little for the group. Or they might work to exclude teammates by dominating discussions, imposing their decisions, and making sure these teammates do not feel welcomed or appreciated so that they withdraw from work. Unfortunately, surveys have found startlingly high rates of employee disengagement from their jobs and active hostility to their managers and colleagues (Hogan, Curphy, and Hogan, 1994; Kouzes and Posner, 2008).

It is not just having individuals work in team settings that make them productive. Many studies indicate that cooperative goals and open-minded discussion help individual team members be motivated and effective in getting things done and supporting each other. Subsequent chapters show how you and your teammates can use this knowledge to develop your team.

A practical theory also stimulates research to document whether and when the proposed conditions have the theorized substantial impact. Evidence bolsters the confidence that, when we create these relationships and interactions, team members are much more likely to work together productively. Theory proposes, but research needs to document.

A practical theory is also shared; team members can together study and learn the theory so that they can collectively use this to analyze their team and identify strengths and ways to improve it. Teams are more effective when every member contributes. All members ought to have a clear and common understanding of how they should work together.

Our model of productive teamwork is not a great theory as it can be improved to make it more powerful and credible. Fortunately, a good theory can be very practical.

Model of Productive Teamwork

Our model identifies two vital complementary conditions: Cooperative goals and open-minded discussion. Team members who develop cooperative relationships are also able to discuss their various ideas openly and constructively. Discussing ideas open-mindedly reaffirms cooperative goals. With cooperative goals and open-mindedness, teams have been found to complete important projects as well as strengthen themselves and their relationships.

Cooperative Goals

Cooperative goals identify the kind of relationships team members should develop that provide the foundation for productive collaboration. Team members should believe that they could reach their goals if and only if other team members also reach their goals. Their self-interests are positively related: as one team member succeeds, others also succeed.

In cooperation, team members have their own goals but they understand that their goals are positively linked. As one teammate reaches his or her goals, that helps others to reach their goals. They feel that they are "in this together." They want each other to succeed and they recognize that as one succeeds, others do too. The situation is "win–win" where team members achieve their goals together. They may, for example, have a common task they are all recognized for accomplishing and for which they all receive a reward.

Cooperative goals are so useful because they encourage people to assist each other and exchange their resources so that they can all succeed. They help each other because as one achieves what he or she wants, others also achieve what they want.

Open-Minded Discussion

The second condition for effective teamwork is open-minded discussion; it identifies the desired interaction between team members, that is, how they should treat each other and discuss even divisive issues together. Open-minded discussion identifies how team members can talk through issues to manage their own internal concerns and create solutions to accomplish their tasks.

With cooperative goals, team members are poised to assist each other including discussing their various ideas and frustrations openly and constructively. What has proved especially valuable in many situations is that cooperative goals help team members develop and express their own ideas and opposing views.

Cooperative team members discuss their different ideas directly. As they express their own views, they also seek to understand the views of others and work to integrate them into high-quality solutions. These open-minded discussions both solve difficult problems and integrate people so that they feel more committed to the solution and to their team.

When confronted with a problem or decision, teammates typically have an initial conclusion and may be confident in it despite incomplete information and quick analysis. However, when they begin to discuss their ideas, they are confronted with different conclusions based on other people's information, experiences, and perspectives. When they discuss directly and openly with each other, they become less certain about their own views and search for more information and try to understand opposing views.

The expression and defending of various views and the search for more information and understanding lead to the development of innovative solutions to problems. Through understanding and accommodating the perspectives and reasoning of others, people can reorganize their thinking and develop new conclusions that are often superior. The open-minded discussion and the creation of new alternatives lay the foundations for genuine agreement and solutions that team members accept and implement. Teammates may have repeated discussions before an agreement is reached or, indeed, they may be unable to create a solution that is mutually acceptable, for example, when they are unconvinced that the evidence warrants modifying their original positions. Chapter 7 examines open-mindedness in more depth.

Cooperative Goals and Open-Mindedness

Considerable research both in the West and in the East has shown that cooperative goals and open-minded discussion complement each other and very much contribute to productive outcomes. Together cooperative goals and open-minded discussion have been found to result in effective decisions and innovations and to strengthen commitment and motivation to work together.

Cooperative goals and open-minded discussion are fundamental conditions for effective teams but they are not absolute rules. Sometimes they are not practical or desirable. However, for most situations, they help teams to complete complex tasks and strengthen relationships.

Cooperative goals and open-minded discussion really do make a difference. They make teams much more effective in important ways. We do not argue, though, that developing this kind of teamwork is easy. The major purpose of this book is to help you and your teammates strengthen cooperative goals and discuss open-mindedly.

THEORY OF COOPERATION AND COMPETITION

Our model of effective teamwork is based on Deutsch's (1973) theory of cooperation and competition. Understanding the theory helps to use the model effectively and accurately; applying the model also helps to understand the theory.

The theory of cooperation and competition assumes that individuals, as well as groups and organizations, pursue their own goals that they expect will promote their interests and values. However, they are interdependent in that the accomplishment of each individual's goals is affected by the actions of others (Deutsch, 1949, 1973; Johnson and Johnson, 1989, 2005; Johnson, Johnson, and Tjosvold, 2014).

The theory holds that the beliefs of people and organizations about how their goals are related to each other affect the dynamics and consequences of their interaction. The way people's goals are related determines how they interact and how they interact affects the outcomes of their collaboration.

Types of Goal Interdependence

People can reach different conclusions about the nature of their interdependence, specifically, how their goals and self-interests are related to each other. There are three types of interdependence.

Cooperation exists when team members believe that they can reach their goals when others also reach their goals, that is, there is a mutually perceived, positive relationship among goal attainments. As a consequence, team members promote each other's efforts to achieve the goals because as they promote one another's' goals, that helps them achieve their own goals. The effective action of one helps others to be effective.

Competition occurs when team members believe that they can obtain their goals if and only if the other team members fail to obtain their goals, that is, there is a negative relationship among goal attainments. Therefore, they are tempted to obstruct each other's efforts to achieve their goals because such obstruction makes it more likely that the obstructer will achieve his or her own goals. The situation is "win–lose" where team members achieve their goals when others fail.

Independence exists when people believe that they can reach their goals without regard for whether others in the situation attain or do not attain their goals. The situation is "do your own thing" where team members achieve or fail their goals alone.

Interaction Patterns

The basic premise of the theory of cooperation and competition is that the way in which goal interdependence is structured determines how team members interact, and the interaction pattern determines the outcomes. Cooperative goals result in team members encouraging and facilitating each other's efforts to complete tasks, achieve, and produce in order to reach positively related goals. As they help the other reach his or her goals, they help themselves reach their own goals. Specifically, cooperative goals promote open-minded discussion for mutual benefit.

Competitive goals result in oppositional interaction, which is defined as team members discouraging and obstructing each other's efforts to complete tasks, achieve, and produce. In competition, these interactions help team members reach their own goals while others fail to reach their goals.

Independence results in little interaction. Team members act separately without exchange as they work to achieve their own goals.

Research on Effects

Considerable research conducted in diverse settings and using various methods has documented the consequences of cooperative and competitive goals on how people interact and the consequences of this interaction. Though mostly collected in the West, this evidence has laid a strong foundation for understanding the effects of goal interdependence (Johnson and Johnson, 2005). This research has been conducted in 12 different historical decades, with widely diverse participants ranging in age from three to post-college adults, with many different operationalizations of cooperation and competition, with a wide variety of dependent measures, conducted in numerous disciplines, and undertaken in many countries and cultures. Laboratory and field studies have both developed the theory; we can be confident of the hypothesized causal relationships and that these relationships hold for a wide variety of situations. Indeed, the literature is one of the largest bodies of research within psychology.

Meta-analyses of the research have examined the effects of cooperation and competition on productivity, relationships, and psychological health. Results indicate that cooperation promotes considerably more productive action and achievement than do competition and independence, and that this difference is large.

Quality of relationships includes such variables as interpersonal attraction, liking, and cohesion. There are over 175 studies that have investigated the relative impact of cooperative, competitive, and individualistic approaches on quality of relationships and another 106 studies on social support (Johnson and Johnson, 1989). Cooperation results in greater interpersonal attraction and greater social support than competition and these effects are also large.

These results confirm popular thinking; for example, they show that developing cooperative goals strengthens the quality of relationships, whereas competition and independence do not. Other findings challenge common theorizing; for example, many researchers and professionals have long assumed that competition promotes achievement and productivity—competition has been lauded as the reason for the success of the free market system. However, these meta-analytic results indicate that, over the range of tasks, populations, and methods studied, promoting cooperative goals strengthens effort and actual productivity compared to competitive and independent goals.

In addition, there is debate about the value of competition and cooperation for furthering self-esteem. It is popular to think that competition builds self-esteem by testing a person's resourcefulness and enterprise. But, results indicate that in most situations, cooperation develops psychological health, and competition does not strengthen self-esteem and can seriously undermine it. Success at competition may not be very affirming, as one has to continue to prove that one is superior to others in order to be confident in oneself.

As it can guide developing interdependence and interaction at various levels, the theory of cooperation and competition has important practical implications. Members of teams, departments, and alliances can use the theory to strengthen their teamwork. There are clear relationships among theory, research, and practice. The more efforts to develop teamwork are directly based on theory, the more effective and the more long-lasting the teamwork will be.

TABLE 2.1   Cooperative, competitive, and independent goals

Goals	Experience	Definitions	Measures	Develop
Cooperative goals	Everyone is trying to achieve the goal of the team. Teammates want to help each other.	Self-interests are positively related. As one team member succeeds, others also succeed.	"Swim or sink" together. Want each other to succeed. Seek compatible goals. Goals go together. Have common goals.	Structure team tasks where everyone is rewarded when task is achieved. Celebrate joint success.
Competitive goals	Worry teammates obstruct their success. Each wants to succeed	Negative relationship among goal attainments. Teammates achieve their goals if and	Structure things in ways that favor their goals rather than others. "Win–lose" relationship.	Criterion for success is outdoing others. Top performer is rewarded, others are not.

Goals	Experience	Definitions	Measures	Develop
	by winning and having others lose.	only if the other team members fail to obtain their goals.	Team members' goals are incompatible. Give high priority to the things they want to accomplish and low priority to the things others want to accomplish.	
Independent goals	One member's work does not affect the work of others. Each succeeds by him or herself.	No relation-ship among goals. Each member reaches their own goals without regard for others.	Succeed through their own individual work. Work for their own independent goals. Successes are unrelated to each other. Get rewards through their own individual work.	Reward for achieving established standards. Reward based on independent performance.

Our model of teamwork uses theory and research to summarize the major conditions that should be created to develop productive teamwork. Considerable research shows that cooperative goals and open-minded discussion promote teamwork, whether on the shop floor or in the boardroom, working to improve manufacturing or high quality customer service, or based in Asia or the West or cross-cultural teams. It is a common, practical guide to help team members to work together to serve their customers, enhance employees, and manage change. The following chapters will help you and your team members understand and apply the model to make your teams effective and meaningful.

Action Plans

Do less of:

- Attribute poor teamwork to a lack of motivation.
- Blame individuals for poor teamwork.
- Assume people know what makes a team effective.
- Believe that cooperation requires altruism.
- Equate avoiding conflict with cooperation.
- Equate competition with high productivity.

Do more of:

- Use theory and research to identify the nature of productive teamwork.
- Study and discuss open-mindedly to develop a common understanding of productive teamwork.
- Employees commit to teamwork after they understand it and its value.
- Employees commit to teamwork when they believe others are committed.
- Understand how cooperative goals support mutual assistance, including open-minded discussion.
- Distinguish cooperation as positively related goals, competition as incompatible goals, and conflict as incompatible actions.
- Understand how cooperation can help people pursue their self-interests and develop their individuality.
- Comprehend specific ways that competitive and independent work frustrates joint work.
- Study how cooperative goals and open-minded discussion can make teams productive.

chapter 3

Applying the Model: The Method Reinforces the Message

For things we have to learn before we do them, we learn by doing them.

Aristotle

The model of cooperative goals and open-minded discussion introduced in Chapter 2 provides a common guide for developing productive teamwork throughout the organization. Employees can use the model to work together to understand, become committed, and strengthen their cooperative teamwork. Team members learn the model through cooperative teamwork and open-minded discussions. The methods to understand and apply the model reinforce the message. As they work together to understand the model, they gain experience in working cooperatively and discussing issues open-mindedly. They have concrete examples of what it means to work as a cooperative team.

Applying the Model: Book Clubs

Book clubs are an important way that our family business uses the model to develop cooperative, open-minded leadership and teamwork throughout the company. Mary, as the chief executive officer (CEO) of the company, offers managers and supervisors from different units within the company the chance to form a book club to read and discuss a teamwork and leadership book, such as one of our own. Before each session, the members of the club read a chapter and prepare to discuss and critique the ideas of the chapter. They also reflect on their own experiences by identifying concrete times when they faced a similar problem. At later sessions, they describe specific times when they have used ideas from the book to strengthen their leadership.

For example, after reading a chapter on managing conflict with an employee, they talk about specific times when they managed conflict with one of their employees. They brainstorm concrete ways that they can apply the chapter's ideas so that they can manage conflict with employees more effectively. At the next meeting, they discuss their attempts to apply the ideas and get suggestions for how to continue and improve their efforts at dealing with conflicts with employees openly and constructively. In these ways, managers and supervisors encourage and provide each other with concrete support to improve their conflict management. Team discussion of ideas, reflecting on experiences, and making commitments for how to improve are powerful ways to learn and become a leader.

Our managers are highly motivated to become leaders who help their employees work as an effective team. But becoming a team leader is very difficult for even motivated people to do alone. Book clubs provide a valuable forum and support for managers to understand, apply, and reflect on ideas as they develop their own way of leading.

Book clubs are important to the organization as well as to the club members. Typically there are several book clubs at any one time. Our family business has a challenging vision that involves teamwork among 800 diverse employees distributed across 50 sites, mostly in Minnesota but also in Arizona and Maryland. We are in the rewarding business of providing residential services for people with special needs, such as homes for people with developmental disabilities and brain injuries, as well as catered, service-assisted living, nursing home, and hospice.

Many employees find the company's vision motivating and their personal work meaningful, yet we need leaders to promote teamwork among nurses, direct service people, managers, accountants, and other specialists. As a service organization, we must also develop team relationships with our clients, their families, and government and non-governmental agencies. Without this teamwork throughout the company, managers and employees easily become frustrated and doubt that they can contribute much to the lives and development of our clients. If that happens, then our motivating vision frustrates rather than motivates. Employees very much want to contribute but are irritated that they cannot effectively promote the development and wellbeing of clients.

The team model provides a common direction for the book clubs, workshops, and discussions throughout the company. Teams meet regularly to reflect on their cooperative goals, open-minded discussion, and related ideas. People throughout the whole organization use the model to have fruitful conversations about their experiences as they develop their teamwork. The model helps everyone have a common understanding of the kind of team organization they want to develop.

Ideally, you, our readers, will follow reading this book by discussing the book's ideas with other professionals. Reading about leadership and teamwork ideas is useful, but discussing and actively thinking about these ideas will deepen your understanding. Your experimentation with applying the book's ideas and getting feedback on your efforts will reinforce your learning and leadership.

How about Dancing?

Vineet Nayar had the vision that he needed to develop HCL as a team organization where together they would serve customers as partners. Providing customers with value and meeting their needs were vital but employees had to come first so that they could deliver. Teamwork was needed to serve customers but teamwork was also needed to develop employees and company offerings so that they could.

Nayar knew that the required teamwork included open discussion and exchange. He also had his methods: He arranged meetings but kept his own talking to a minimum so that people had the opportunity to talk themselves. And he had dancing. His dancing symbolized the new kind of relationships he wanted up and down the organization.

We also dance! Every year residents from various homes come together for a formal dance. They also crown a King and Queen of the Dance. Employees help residents chose their formal wear and beauty salon professionals volunteer to provide new hairstyles and looks. Clients and staff have a great deal of fun together while renewing their friendships and reinforcing teamwork. Dancing and applying the model complement each other.

We do more than dance. Since 1998, Mary has volunteered for the American Refugee Committee that specializes in refugee management and health development. After one of several visits to refugee camps in Asia, our mother took the lead in organizing our employees and community to make sure every child in the refugee camps in Thailand had at least one stuffed animal to sleep with. On visiting Africa, our mother saw that the young children in Santa Bamenda, Cameroon, had no primary school. Since 2001, our employees have contributed by raising funds to build the schoolhouse, pay teachers, and provide supplies. By 2014, the school had grown to 250 students and ten teachers. Mary and company employees pay frequent visits to support the school in such ways as organizing sports days and celebrating graduations. Local communities and the wider world provide many worthwhile projects that stimulate meaningful teamwork.

CROWD SOURCING: TEAM PROBLEM SOLVING ON THE INTERNET

Eliot Higgens, an unemployed blogger based in Leicester England, is credited with documenting to the world that President Assad's forces used chemical weapons against civilians and rebel fighters in Guhouta, Syria (Keefe, 2013). The evidence he gathered meticulously—he sometimes examined

300 videos a day—was so compelling that even the Syrian government moved away from insisting that Syrian opposition was guilty and began to work with the West to reduce and possibly eliminate its chemical weapons.

Higgens played a pivotal role but he had and needed partners inside and outside Syria to provide the considerable evidence necessary to confirm the rockets used in the attack and from where they were fired. For example, he asked Syrians at the site to provide photos with a measuring tape to document the length of the rocket. This evidence, along with many other sources, identified the kind of Soviet-made rockets used in the attack.

He had an open-minded, team approach to the evidence. He listened, often through YouTube videos, to the Syrian opposition arguments holding Assad responsible, but he asked them for evidence. He also followed the government's arguments and YouTube contributions because they might provide evidence. Unwittingly, they showed that the Syrian government had the kind of rockets used in the attack.

Higgens was also open with his own evidence. He listed the evidence that he had collected and offered to send what his readers requested to them.

Other bloggers were not rivals but partners with a common, vital task of documenting who was responsible. Higgens was not committed to showing that he was right; he was committed that the world should know who was responsible for the attack. His and his partners' goal was that their success would dissuade other warriors that they can use chemical weapons with impunity.

Not speaking Arabic and building upon his weapons knowledge, he wanted technical evidence especially about weaponry, not just opinions and conclusions. For example, he was able to access five images of the site where the rockets landed and spread gas. Using the shadows displayed on the photos and the times the photos were taken, along with other evidence, he determined that the rockets were fired from 6 to 8 kilometers north of Guhouta, an area where the Assad government has military bases.

Higgens' crowd sourcing demonstrates the potential of teamwork enabled by the Internet. Participants from around the world are able to collect and combine a great variety of evidence and arguments to solve problems that individuals alone or even teams that are in one place cannot. Like other teams, crowd sourcing must be effectively managed to yield quality results—after the Boston marathon bombing, crowd sourcing identified several innocent men.

Developing cooperative goals and open-minded discussion can be quite challenging in crowd sourcing. Participants are likely to have different goals and be unsure whether their goals are positively or negatively related to each other. The Syrian government suspected Higgens and other Western-based bloggers and intelligence personnel and did not voluntarily contribute helpful evidence. Higgens and the Syrian rebels had different goals; the rebels wanted to blame the Assad government. Higgens told rebels that he might be able to help them but his goal was to use technical weapons information to document the perpetuators of the crime whoever they are. Before he could help them, they had to help him develop the evidence.

Open-minded discussion is also needed for effective crowd sourcing. Crowd sourcing has considerable potential because it can integrate the various views and knowledge of many diverse people. Higgens recognized that the Internet distributes a lot of misleading information as well as accurate evidence.

Higgens wanted to rely on incontrovertible technical weapons information. The United States intelligence community's reliance on false information to justify the invasion of Iraq had very much affected his approach to crowd sourcing. He would not rely on the opinions of sources, but asked them to strengthen their positions through more evidence on the weapons used.

Higgens was instrumental in documenting that the Assad government had violated international law and committed a heinous crime against its own people. Future combatants should be aware that they would be held accountable for committing such a crime against humanity. However, he recognized that he could succeed only by developing cooperative relationships with a diverse group of partners who could open-mindedly share information and challenge each other's thinking and evidence.

Learning and Applying the Model Together

Developing cooperative goals and open-minded discussion is easy to say but difficult to do. A combined consideration of research on training and cooperation and competition with professional practice suggests three major parts for using the model to develop cooperative teamwork.

Team Members

1. Study and talk: Have teams read and discussed the model? Team members understand the model, appreciate the value of cooperative goals and open-minded discussion, and learn methods to strengthen them.
2. Debate and decide: Use open discussion to analyze and critique the model. In addition to understanding its value, people express their misgivings about the model and the effort needed to develop teamwork. Through open-minded discussion, teams order their priorities and develop practical ways to improve their cooperative teamwork. This participation in discussing teamwork can improve the quality of the decisions on how they should develop cooperative teamwork and their commitment to these decisions.
3. Reflect and develop: Reflect on experiences and learn from them. Team members assess and receive feedback on their teamwork and develop concrete ways to strengthen cooperative teamwork. Reflecting skillfully on experiences strengthens teamwork.

Teams accomplish goals that no individual can. But they also require understanding, investment, and ongoing maintenance. The more you invest in your teams, the more you receive.

Study and Discuss

A favorite way for us to have team members learn about cooperation and controversy is the jigsaw method. We begin by forming small teams. Teams of four persons are ideal. Then we divide each small team into sub-groups with each subgroup sitting face-to-face. One subgroup is assigned to study and learn about cooperative goals and the other, open-minded discussion. Each group is given readings—for example, material from this book—on their part. Each subgroup has the common goals of helping each member understand their part and being prepared to teach this part to a person learning the other part. After they are confident that they understand their part of the model and can teach it, new two-person groups are formed, each with one person who has studied cooperative goals and one who has studied open-minded discussion.

After both persons have presented their teaching lessons and answered questions, they reform their original teams of four and have an open-minded discussion about the model. They identify strengths and uses of the model: How would the model help and where should they begin to apply it? Emphasis is placed on understanding and appreciating the model. Later they critique and discuss its limitations.

Jigsaw is one method to meet the first challenge of having a clear under-standing of these concepts. Just reading about an idea is seldom enough to grasp significant ideas like cooperation and open-minded discussion in much depth.

In Dean's MBA class in Shanghai, a mature student could not understand nor accept the research on the constructive outcomes of cooperation compared to competition. He based his strong feelings in large part on the bonus system that he experienced in his company in Columbia, South

America. The student argued that the program undoubtedly worked well and he was convinced it was effective because of the competition in the reward system. Moreover, salespeople tended to help each other; competition did not seem to get in the way of mutual support, as Dean suggested.

As a teacher, Dean encourages these debates because feeling strongly about management issues helps build motivation to learn. These discussions can also lead to alternative ways of talking about the ideas that can help all students understand the ideas better. However, after various activities and discussions, the Columbian student had not changed or altered his positions; he kept re-stating the same arguments in the same way. Dean (finally) asked him to describe in detail the reward system with its bonuses. His description made it clear that these bonuses were based on a combination of individual achievement and team performance as measured by the sales volume of the whole store. Front-line salespeople received a quarterly performance bonus based both on their own sales volume and that of the store.

The system had no competitive rewards. Individual salespersons who performed well were rewarded but everyone was rewarded when other salespeople performed well too. The Columbian student had read and discussed cooperation and competition but had not understood. As we learned about his company's bonus system and reviewed the definitions, he understood that he was using the term competition loosely. For him, competition meant high motivation and effective performance. High aspirations and wanting to do well are different ideas than competition as negatively related goals.

After he clarified his confusion, the student became less "stuck" on his beliefs and more open. He began to understand more about the theory and research on cooperation and competition. This incident reinforced to Dean the notion that accurate understanding of concepts is critical but not easily attained, even for bright, experienced students. Team members, instructors, and students may all be saying "competition" but have different meanings for it.

TEAMS FOR LEARNING

Educational researchers have documented that learning ideas so that they can be applied is much more difficult than often assumed (Halpern and Hakel, 2002). They have argued, for example, that most professors try to "cover" too many topics and ideas in their university classrooms; they have called on them to focus on a few central ideas in depth so that students learn and apply ideas.

Learning is often associated with listening and reading, but a great deal of research has underlined the value of people talking about and explaining as they learn ideas. Studies document that people learn ideas more thoroughly by active participation than passive reading or listening to lectures. People learn by discussing their understandings and questions with instructors, of course, but also by talking with other participants in workshops and classrooms. Considerable evidence indicates that cooperative teams encourage the active involvement and discussion that help each individual in the team to learn complex ideas. Findings indicate that individuals in cooperative groups have higher achievement than those learning in competitive and independent situations (Johnson, Druckman, and Dansereau, 1994).

In helping people learn more about cooperative goals, team training has the important advantage that building cooperative groups facilitates the training goals. Team members become more knowledgeable about cooperation and open-minded discussion as they learn about them in teams. Discussing the ideas together and working to apply ideas to their team promotes learning about teamwork.

Ideally, team members consider and discuss this book's ideas together; they develop their own book club. They study, explain, and debate the ideas as they read chapters. They also plan and carry out experiments about how they can apply their ideas in their own situations. In this way, the method reinforces the message: They become an effective team as they learn about teamwork together.

Debate and Decide

Team members deepen their understanding of the team model through challenging and disputing it. In the jigsaw method described above, people discuss and disagree as they learn their part of the model and as they teach each other their parts. After they have focused on understanding, we encourage teams to discuss the model open-mindedly. They identify strengths and uses of the model and what they like about the model; they also discuss their questions, doubts, and misgivings, their "yes, buts." Although there is always the danger that people will criticize ideas before they understand them, evaluating ideas is constructive after a good effort to understand them.

The model is powerful in that it is abstract and applies across many kinds of teams but, as a consequence, it does not offer a concrete plan for how teamwork should be developed and maintained. Open-minded discussion among team members is useful for developing quality solutions to such questions as how much time and resources to invest in teamwork. Teamwork is not costly compared to building a new plant but it is costly in that people need to invest in learning and developing their teams.

Advocacy team method is one way to stimulate discussion about what the organization should do. Chapter 6 describes advocacy teams more fully and Chapter 11 provides an example of how to implement them.

In addition to deciding whether to invest in teamwork and how much to invest, team members can also help develop concrete plans for how to invest. For larger groups, employees are selected to a steering team that considers and recommends next steps. These steps might be workshops on particular aspects of teamwork, book clubs to develop team leaders, and visits to other organizations.

Reflect and Develop

Teams are not machines made at one time that then run merrily along. They inevitably have hitches and hiccups. Members should assess their teamwork and develop concrete ways to deal with issues and strengthen their teamwork.

Managers and employees reflect on their relationships regardless of whether they have a teamwork program. They confide in spouses, friends, and therapists. At lunch, over drinks after work, and in the hallway, they turn to talking about their relationships. They describe and analyze, complain and criticize, praise and thank.

Teams should use the energy and emotion of discussing relationships to good effect. Reflection should become a regular, public feature of how teams operate. Team members openly and periodically take stock of themselves and their situation. They assess their cooperative goals and open-mindedness and make realistic plans to improve. Teams need adjusting, nurturing, and strengthening.

Fortunately, cooperative relationships are a solid basis upon which to develop teamwork, in part because they stimulate useful feedback that fosters learning. Team members have been found to be more accepting, open, and respectful of feedback when they are working cooperatively rather than competitively (Tjosvold, Tang, and West, 2004). Cooperative goals help teams reflect on their experiences effectively and to learn from their experiences and mistakes (Tjosvold, Yu, and Hui, 2004; Tjosvold, Tang, and West, 2004).

The teamwork model is like a good recipe that identifies the general plan and then inspires cooks to use their talents and own ingredients to make a unique dish. The next section reviews how companies have used the model to strengthen their teamwork and customer service.

Field Experiments on Applying the Model

Cooperation and competition studies complement training research to identify conditions that develop cooperative teamwork (Johnson et al., 1994). Together these studies indicate that effective training requires employees to be motivated and knowledgeable about cooperative ideas and behaviors, actively participate in the training, be trained as a cohort, and engage in ongoing development and feedback. Cooperative teams facilitate training a wide range of desirable behavior, including teamwork (Johnson et al., 1994).

Experiments have demonstrated how to develop cooperative teamwork in different companies by carefully monitoring the processes and measuring the outcomes. These experiments followed the steps of study and discuss, debate and decide, and reflect and develop.

High Tech in Beijing

Teams in a high technology company based in Beijing were trained during a weekend cooperative team workshop and two-month follow-up of team feedback and discussion (Lu, Tjosvold, and Shi, 2010). Over 150 employees from all the teams in the company participated in the weekend workshop. For two months they reflected on their teamwork to develop more effective ways of working together. The design allowed for measuring the effects of the workshop and follow-up activities on the relationships and interactions between the teams as well as within the teams.

The results of this training support the idea that teams can use the productive teamwork model to strengthen their internal functioning, collaboration among teams, and contributions to their organization. Specifically, the findings indicate that the cooperative teamwork training heightened beliefs that goals were positively related, fostered task-focused open-minded discussion, promoted creative processes across teams as well as within them, and resulted in higher group productivity and potency. The teamwork model identifies conditions and dynamics by which teams can effectively contribute to their organization and is a basis upon which teamwork throughout an organization can be developed.

Call Centers for Quality Customer Service

A second training program demonstrated that developing cooperative teamwork could help employees improve their individual performance and manage stress productively (Tjosvold, Chen, Huang, and Xu, 2014).

Three hundred and sixty-eight employees in a call center were placed in groups of six and participated in a day workshop. They then engaged in development activities for two months.

Teams met for five to ten minutes before and after their shifts and once a week for an hour. They discussed both their successful interactions with customers and their frustrating experiences with harassing, hostile callers. They vented their feelings but also identified how they could handle similar cases more effectively in the future. They also made plans for how they can relax and get prepared for work. Every two weeks, they met with another team to share their experiences and to broaden their social network. Many groups enjoyed meals and short trips together on weekends.

Results after two months were impressive. In addition to strengthening their relationships and attitudes toward each other, team members also improved their individual customer service. They increased the number of phones answered by nearly 40 per cent, shrunk customer complaints by over 55 per cent, and reduced the call center's turnover by over 20 per cent in two months. Cooperative teamwork helped employees feel more integrated into their work, reduced service errors, and improved customer service. Cooperative teamwork can make individuals stronger both in their attitudes and job performance.

Cooperative Teamwork to Socialize Newcomers

Teams must adjust and adapt as they include and socialize new members. Newcomer studies indicate that a team climate that encourages cooperation among team members helps newcomers feel part of a team and learn how to do their jobs. An experimental study conducted in Beijing with 90 university students found that developing a cooperative team climate, compared to a competitive or independent climate, strengthened the relationship and interaction between newcomers and team members and, thereby, facilitated newcomer respect and trust towards the senior teammates as well as job satisfaction and sense of belonging to the team (Chen, Lu, Tjosvold, and Lin, 2008).

Middle managers newly recruited into a large telecom company in China indicated that teams that valued relationships and open discussion, compared to not valuing relationships and avoiding open discussion, facilitated their socialization and strengthened cooperative goals in their teams (Chen, Tjosvold, Huang, and Xu, 2011). Team members, when they were inclusive and helpful to newcomers, developed cooperative goals that resulted in effective newcomer socialization (Lu and Tjosvold, 2013). Applying the teamwork model can help teams adjust to membership changes and include newcomers.

Understanding and applying the model of cooperative goals and open-minded discussion helps teams get things done as well as making their teamwork more personally rewarding. But productive teamwork requires investment. Team members can study the model together, debate and experiment with applying the model, and reflect on their experiences to improve their teamwork. Learning the model helps to apply it; applying the model helps to learn it.

Action Plans

Do less of:

- Try to impose cooperative goals and open-minded discussions.
- Skip understanding teamwork, emphasize action only.
- Skip action to develop teamwork, emphasize understanding only.
- Suppress discussions about frustrations with working in teams.

Do more of:

- Study and apply teamwork ideas together.
- Use jigsaw and other methods so that team members discuss and learn the teamwork model together.
- Discuss the pros and cons of investing in teamwork.
- Understand how the teamwork model provides a common guide to strengthen teams and organizations.
- Understand why teamwork should be continuously strengthened.
- Use teams to support employee learning.
- Form book clubs to deepen understanding of teamwork and leadership.

4
Getting Started

Knowing is not enough; we must apply. Willing is not enough; we must do.

Goethe

Team leaders and members can use the cooperative goals open-mindedness model to develop a common vision of the kind of team they want to be. To realize the potential of their team, team members should develop efficient ways to strengthen their cooperative relationships and open-minded discussions.

This chapter complements the previous chapters by suggesting concrete steps that employees and managers can take to begin, form, and manage their cooperative, open-minded teams. It addresses practical issues, such as:

- "How can we get started?"
- "Who should be on our team?"
- "How many members are optimal?"

The team model and research, although not providing specific answers to these questions, help team leaders and members develop plans that are appropriate and effective for their team and situation. Team leaders and members must use their own judgments and consider practical concerns as they apply the team model.

Team Tasks and Purposes

Developing the right kind of task for teams is a powerful way to lay the foundations for productive teamwork. This section shows that team tasks should be common, meaningful, challenging, and achievable. Common tasks that members are committed to are important ways to strengthen cooperative goals. Ideally, members should also find these tasks meaningful to them; they can see where these tasks are useful for others as well as themselves. Team tasks should challenge members and require that they apply and develop each other's abilities. But teams should also believe that, with effort, they could successfully complete the task.

Tasks often seem like "givens," beyond the control of managers and employees. But typically leaders and members can use their own discretion to construct their tasks. Organizations have traditionally assigned tasks to individuals; now they increasingly assign tasks to teams. Tasks can be considered in broad ways, such as handling crises that might emerge in the company, or in more focused ways, such as handling a specific customer's complaint.

Our call center field experiment changed and enlarged the task assigned to individual operators (Tjosvold, Chen, Huang, and Xu, 2012). Before the experiment, their task was to answer their own calls efficiently; our study added the task to help each other learn from their experiences and improve the effectiveness of each team member's customer call handling. Having this common task helped the teams develop cooperative relationships, discuss issues open-mindedly, and reduce service errors committed by individuals.

Common tasks that are meaningful for members are especially useful for strengthening cooperative goals. Call center employees were motivated in part because they wanted to share their experiences, learn from each other, and improve their performance. They also wanted to be friends who help each other develop their capabilities. Having meals together and sharing team awards highlighted that they taught and encouraged each other.

Learning was a particularly meaningful and valuable common task for the call center's teams. Learning can also strengthen many other team tasks. For example, work teams are not only expected to develop efficient ways to use new technology but also to help members understand potential future technology and develop their abilities to communicate and work together. They not only learn but also develop their skills in helping others learn (Johnson and Johnson 2005; Johnson, Maruyama, Johnson, Nelson, and Skon, 1981).

Tasks that challenge team members also motivate. David McClelland (1987) found that difficult tasks are particularly rich for meeting achievement needs. Although some people have higher achievement needs than others, we all have needs to do well comparatively to standards of excellence; we want to perform effectively for the internal satisfaction of getting the job done at a high standard of quality. Accomplishing challenging tasks allows us to feel successful. These tasks can also be socially rewarding, as other people recognize our achievement.

Challenging tasks are particularly useful for teams. Members recognize that, in addition to applying their own individual abilities, they need the assistance, ideas, and support of others to complete the task. For example, call center employees individually responded to most inquiries but consulted each other on difficult calls.

Individuals can easily and with justification believe that they can do simple tasks efficiently by working alone without the need to coordinate. They may even be tempted to compete by showing their boss and others that they can do the tasks more efficiently than others.

That teams are assigned tasks is sometimes mistaken to mean that individuals and their motivation and efforts are unimportant. But it is individuals who get things done. With team tasks, individuals recognize that their part needs to be supplemented and enhanced by the actions of team members. Indeed, teams should hold individuals accountable for completing their assignments and making sure they coordinate with those of their teammates.

A major advantage of teams is that they can place considerable pressure on members to be responsible. Combatant soldiers often report that they are fighting more for their platoon than for their country. Wanting to be recognized and valued, teammates are very open to each other's suggestions and requests. Team tasks that are common, meaningful, and challenging make it more likely that social pressure will be exerted so that individuals will work together to get things done.

Small Size is Useful

Team tasks should be challenging but that does not mean that you should structure tasks that require an army of people. The basic guide for team size is small. Think small, even real small; consider forming groups of two, three, and four people. The basic reason is that although larger groups have more resources, it is much easier for small groups to coordinate their efforts and integrate their ideas. Members can more easily identify and use each other's resources and abilities than those in large groups. They can also get to know each other better and develop ways of working with each more easily in small than in large groups.

We think it is easy for managers and other team leaders to fail to appreciate the challenges of coordinating, particularly as the group gets larger. They believe that team members, especially as they might be "similar" in background or have common experiences, can work together with ease. But each person is unique. Each new member of the team is different from the other team members. Team members must get to know each other and adjust to each other. Getting to know each other and developing good working relationships are often highly rewarding, but they are not easily accomplished.

We realize, though, that there are many tasks that are beyond two, three, or four people, indeed, including most tasks in organizations. A human resources (HR) team may develop a new 360-degree feedback program but then they have to work with others to implement it. And many important tasks—new product development, for example—require people with diverse capabilities.

However, teams can still be small. Consider having a team of teams; indeed, an organization is a team of teams. Members can feel included, arrange sessions, coordinate their efforts, and combine ideas effectively in their small groups. But then develop another team, again preferably a small one, where representatives of all the teams coordinate to complete the overall task.

Some tasks may seem to require a large group. But remember, tasks can be modified and it might be prudent to spend effort to re-consider the task so that a small team can manage it. Working in a cooperative team, even a small one, is a rich and interesting experience, but the difficulties and costs with working a large team can be frustrating and disruptive.

Diverse Membership

Who should be included in a team? The simply stated guide is diversity; chose team members who are different from each other. If everyone has similar abilities, perspectives, and experiences, then what is the value of the team for getting things done? Teams are so useful because they encourage the coordination and combination of various abilities and efforts.

Specialists that are relevant for the tasks should be included in the team. Highly trained people are useful for organizations when they combine their ideas and perspectives in conjunction with others. Teams promote and utilize specialization. People studying specialized areas should also study teamwork! "Lone geniuses" do not by themselves have much constructive impact in organizations.

Cross-functional teams, such as new product teams, are popular in organizations because many tasks require solutions that work for the organization as a whole. Engineers must develop the new product, production specialists have to make it, marketing people must sell it, and finance people have to support the investment. Cross-functional teams provide a setting where they can express their various perspectives and work to integrate them so that, to the extent possible, the product can be successful for the company.

A major value of diversity is that, as the model summarizes, teams should have various ideas and opinions to make high quality decisions. Having a team of people with various functional training and life experience makes it more likely that they will create innovative solutions. Diversity makes jumping to the conclusion that everyone agrees less likely. Their conflicts can help dig into problems, understand each other's perspectives, and integrate ideas.

Personal Relationships: Get to Know Your Teammates

Personal relationships reinforce cooperative goals and facilitate coordination and open discussion. Teammates who know each other are in a good position to promote each other and their goals; they understand each other's aspirations and hopes. Understanding each other's personal aspirations can convince everyone that teammates are really committed to the team's tasks.

To facilitate coordination, people who know each other as individuals can read each other's moods and thereby appreciate when and how they can discuss issues so that they are open and responsive to each other. They recognize each other's intentions and meanings accurately. Knowing other people helps us enjoy them more and be able to adjust to their style. As we take each other's perspective, we are more open and less evaluative and judgmental; we come to understand that people have reasons for their thinking and actions.

However, assigning personal friends in a team is often undesirable. In our classes and workshops, we never allow people to choose their own teams, unless they are being trained in their own work group.

It's true that close personal friends can typically develop cooperative goals quickly and thoroughly; they already believe that they are trying to help each other succeed. But before including friends, consider the following. If only two people are friends out of four, what will happen to the other two? Two friends can easily dominate and alienate the other two. The two friends, or even if all team members are friends, may have built their friendships in non-work ways. We like it when our employees become friends as they relax and fish together. However, they may be very committed to ways of interacting that while fine for fishing are not very useful for getting the present task done.

Beginning the team without friends allows people to develop their relationships around the team tasks assigned to them. They become convinced that they have cooperative goals and develop open-minded ways of working with each other that are appropriate and useful for completing their organizational assignment. They can become friends as they become teammates. Perhaps then they will want to go fishing together to celebrate success after they have worked on their tasks.

We are not suggesting that organizations assign employees the task of becoming friends as if their goal is to become personal friends. Organizations are credible in asking employees to complete a task useful for the organization but becoming friends is a decision for employees. Well-structured teams give employees opportunities to become friends, but it is not necessary that they become friends to work together productively. Deciding to be a friend is a personal decision.

Knee-to-Knee, Eye-to-Eye: Key for Team Communication

Knee-to-knee, eye-to-eye is the most important guide for the layout of the meeting. Simply put, people who are coordinating with each other should be sitting face-to-face. They move their chairs so that their knees and eyes face each other directly. Sitting side-by-side, as in a theater, is not knee-to-knee, eye-to-eye!

In a group of three or four, knee-to-knee, eye-to-eye means the members sit in a circle, ideally without any table between them. If it is imperative to have more people at a meeting, then use the smaller is better principle, by breaking the group into teams of two, three, or four so that the meeting is conducted as a team of teams.

Knee-to-knee, eye-to-eye makes communicating, coordinating, and getting to know each other much easier. Then people can see each other's nonverbal messages as well as communicate that they are listening to each other. Human beings have relied upon face-to-face communication for thousands of years; we have practiced, we are used to it.

But what about emails and virtual teams? Of course our technology helps us coordinate across distances from one building to the next, from one country to another. These technologies can really extend and contribute to teamwork. However, we are better at knee-to-knee, eye-to-eye communication.

Every time you are in an airport you can see the appeal of working knee-to-knee, eye-to-eye. Many business people, although they have email, telephones, and video conferencing, are willing to fly many miles so that they can be knee-to-knee, eye-to-eye with their customers, suppliers, bosses, and teammates. When people are already in one room, arranging them to be in small circles is a wise investment in communication!

Forming small groups to develop knee-to-knee, eye-to-eye communication is very useful; but you can expect to meet resistance. Dean once led a group discussion as part of a team rewards conference at Harvard University where he asked the participants to break into two small groups. Richard Hackman, a prominent group theorist whose height matched his wonderful sense of humor, objected that Dean was disrupting an excellent conversation; he did not want to change. But Dean insisted. Ten minutes later when they were asked to reform into one group, Richard again objected that his excellent conversation was being disrupted. Sometimes leaders need a little courage to implement good ideas.

SAVING BABIES: ONE EYE-TO-EYE, KNEE-TO-KNEE RELATIONSHIP AT A TIME

Tragic high newborn death rates have stimulated public health care professionals, governments, and charities to devote considerable resources to saving babies in less developed countries. The Better Birth Project in India has learned that developing personal, knee-to-knee, eye-to-eye, cooperative relationships between professionals and birth nurses is key to making their program effective (Gawande, 2013).

High newborn mortality is not due to the lack of expensive technology and modern drugs, but the result of failure to follow basic principles carefully and consistently. For example, many babies in India get too cold. Even in the United States, half the babies arriving for intensive care are hypothermic. Cold leaves babies very vulnerable.

A generally powerful solution is readily available: swaddle the baby and place the baby on the warm skin of the mother. But the Better Birth Project professionals found that it was not enough to tell and sell this solution to birthing nurses. They had to develop relationships with birthing nurses, who were then prepared to change their thinking and habits and, in turn, to change those of the mothers.

Professionals had to convince birthing nurses that cold is a real, but invisible, threat to newborns; babies do not have to look blue to be too cold. Nurses should take the newborn's temperature properly and frequently. They should be confident enough to confront mothers' thinking and teach them skills. Mothers have to understand that next to their warm bodies is the best place for their baby and learn to swaddle their baby properly.

While these changes may seem straightforward, they require nurses and mothers to discard their old ways and thinking as well as adopt new ones. They had to believe that they not only could change, but that these changes would be more useful than the practices they had thought effective. Nurses also had to incorporate the new ways of taking temperatures and swaddling the newborn into their practice; the nurses would do it correctly for one newborn only to return to their old ways with the next one. In addition to teaching, Better Birth professionals needed to show specifically when and how each nurse could adopt the new practices. They had to encourage nurses but also point out when they left the baby vulnerable.

Nurses had to trust the Better Birth professionals in order to discard some practices and incorporate new ones. They had to believe that the professionals were on their side and become convinced that the new ways and their feedback would pay off. Professionals and nurses had to communicate knee-to-knee, eye-to-eye to develop personal, cooperative, learning relationships that saved babies.

Develop Enhancing Norms

Norms are usually implicit rules about how people expect to treat each other and work together. They are concrete forms of a group's culture; they indicate what the group values in its everyday work. Norms vary from one setting to another; norms for the concert hall are different than the dance hall. Norms for most theaters prescribe that the audience listens attentively; for most dance halls, the norms are that you participate actively and loudly. Theatergoers will give you disapproving looks and more if you dance there, but your dancing at the dancing hall will gain you admirers. Norms are understandings of behaviors that are appropriate and useful in that situation.

Norms vary from one team and one organization to another. As they are so much a part of an organization, norms often seem like they are givens, that they are part of the stable values not subject to change.

However, teams can forget their own norms. The model of productive teamwork provides a guide for developing norms that strengthen and reinforce the team. Agreed upon norms are especially useful for new recruits, so that they can see rather than guess the team's expectations.

Norms can be posted in workrooms and discussed and modified in meetings to make them current and as constructive as possible. Procedures for getting the team to develop norms are:

1. Team members working alone develop norms that they want for their team.
2. The team together develops a common list of norms from these suggestions.
3. Post the norms and distribute the norms to each member.
4. At future meetings, team members discuss how they have profitably used their norms and whether they want to modify the list.

The following norms, based on the model of productive teamwork, might help your team think about its own. Be sure to discuss and adapt these norms to make them suitable and useful for the team.

1. We respect and show our respect to each person.
2. We are punctual.
3. We practice good phone etiquette.
4. We encourage everyone to express his or her ideas.
5. We listen to everyone's ideas, even if we don't agree.
6. We criticize ideas, not people.
7. We re-state other's ideas and feelings to demonstrate that we understand them.
8. We first disagree and then try to integrate.
9. We change our minds when the evidence warrants it.
10. We work to find solutions that are mutually beneficial.
11. We remember we are all in this together.
12. We follow the golden rule of teamwork: We act towards others, as we want them to act to us. For example, if we want them to listen to us, then we listen to them.

Coordinate: Team Meetings!

First, the bad news: Meetings are needed, as they can be effective mechanisms for team coordination. The good news: Meetings can be lively, personal, productive, and brief. Further good news is that the guides to getting your team started—common tasks, small size, personal relationships, and explicit norms—lay the foundation of effective meetings.

Meetings should reinforce team ways of working and strengthen cooperative goals and open-minded discussions. If meetings do not, then they not only waste time, they disrupt and weaken the group. Unfortunately, meetings are often frustrating, as there has not been much teambuilding and people do not feel like a team.

Team members often find it useful to meet briefly, even just five or ten minutes, at the beginning of a workday to greet each other, find out each other's current feelings and issues, identify what each hopes to accomplish, and any special needs to coordinate. Brief meetings at the end of a day help team members let each other know what they accomplished, barriers that they encountered, and team issues that need focused consideration. Members can also say goodbye and share ideas about how they can relax, relieve stress, and get prepared for work the next day.

It is typically a good idea for teams to meet regularly—for example, weekly—to reflect upon and build their teamwork. The emphasis should be on strengthening teamwork rather than waiting for people to get frustrated and call for crisis management.

Below are elements that could be included in an agenda for a 90-minute weekly meeting to discuss issues and coordinate, which also builds the team.

- Opening: ten minutes
  - Team members welcome each other.
  - Each member identifies a feeling to describe their current mood and others respond to people's feelings as appropriate.

- Team members get to know each other better as individuals. For example, each discusses an aspect of himself that is not directly related to work, such as his favorite movie and why it is his favorite movie.
- Strengthening individual performance: 15 minutes
  - Each person describes at least one incident during the past week where they were able to work effectively; they include who was involved, what happened, what the results were, and how they felt about the work. Team members appreciate the efforts and skills that the member demonstrated and developed through the incident.
  - Each member identifies a frustrating incident and describes who was involved, what happened, what the results were, and how they felt about the work. Team members appreciate the efforts and skills that the member demonstrated and developed through the incident.
  - Team members summarize their learning from discussing both satisfying and frustrating incidents.
- Coordinating work: 50 minutes
  - The team brainstorms coordination issues to be discussed and then orders them in terms of their importance and timeliness. Some issues only deserve five-minute discussions; spending too long on unimportant issues must be ranked high on the most frustrating aspect of meetings. Special sessions are arranged to tackle critical, complex problems.
- Reflect on their teamwork: ten minutes
  - Team members reflect on how they work together as a team. They identify three things that they like about how they worked together this week and one way they could improve how they worked together.
  - The team gives each member positive feedback about how he or she has contributed to the team.
- Closing the meeting: five minutes
  - Team members help each person get ready to relax and enjoy their time away from work; they discuss plans to relax, exercise, and other ways to manage stress.

- Team members thank each other for their help and friendship throughout the week!

The team might decide that an important and timely issue needs a special session where people discuss opposing positions in depth. Indeed, some issues and decisions need a great deal of consideration and hard-hitting debate, more than is possible at a weekly teambuilding meeting. Chapter 6 describes concrete ways, such as advocacy teams, to foster open-minded discussion in order to help find solutions to important, complex problems the team faces.

Keeping Records

Some meetings are required to keep formal minutes. But even if not required, a written journal is a useful way to summarize and remember the team's development. In addition to helping the team keep track of its progress and learning, managers can review the folder to understand the team and its needs more thoroughly. HR personnel can use the folder to understand teams better and also to consider how to suggest changes in team and organization procedures.

Team members should take turns keeping the brief written records of their meetings. For example, the group member whose birthday is coming up next could be the first recorder for the first week. Then the group member whose birthday is coming up next is the recorder for the second week, and so on until everyone has been a recorder, then repeat the rotation. You must first find out each other's birthdays, but not necessarily the year of birth!

The record for the weekly coordination teambuilding meeting described above could include:

Date:

Recorder:

1. Team members' feelings.
2. Activity to get to know each other better as individuals.

3. Capabilities team members demonstrate in their discussion of incidents.
4. Frustrating incidents for team members.
5. Learning from discussing satisfying and frustrating incidents.
6. Coordination issues discussed.
7. Decisions taken.
8. Things that team members like about how they worked together this week and ways that they could improve on how they worked together.
9. Plans to relax and enjoy their time away from work.

Enjoying and Naming Your Team

Teamwork requires discipline so that people work together now and in the future. Individuals do not just do their own thing. Managers, team leaders, and team members must work continually to make their team productive and enhancing. Team members should become committed to common tasks and mutual benefit. They should discuss their differences open-mindedly. They should reflect on their experiences and work steadily to improve. They must work continually to coordinate. Teams give a lot, but require a lot.

However, discipline does not mean that team members do not express their own personalities. Indeed, teamwork encourages individuals to build and use their diverse knowledge and specialization so that they can make their teams more resourceful and productive. Teams should be places where individuals speak out and diversity flourishes. Indeed, teams develop their own unique style and ways of working; being in one team is not like being in another team.

Your team may want to develop its own name. Your name can show the personalities of team members and the character of the team. It can also let people know that teammates are serious about their work and team, but also laugh and have fun together.

Action Plans

Do less of:

- Assume members will naturally have cooperative goals.
- Form large teams so that there are plentiful resources.
- Have team members sit shoulder-to-shoulder in a line.
- Have only friends in a team.
- Form teams of like-minded people.

Do more of:

- Form diverse teams.
- Members get to know each other as individual persons.
- Assign common tasks to a team.
- Keep teams small to facilitate coordination.
- Communicate knee-to-knee, eye-to-eye.
- Make meetings involving and concise.
- Develop norms that clarify how members want to work together productively.
- Keep records of team development.
- Enjoy naming teams in a way that lets others know each team and its individual members.

Building Team Relationships

The only irreplaceable capital an organization possesses is the knowledge and ability of its people; the productivity of that capital depends on how effectively people share their competence with those who can use it.

Andrew Carnegie

5

Leadership for Teamwork, Teamwork for Leadership

Managers work with and through others to get things done.
Traditional saying

Joel, Senior Vice President for Customer Relationships at Community Bank, was brooding about that morning's meeting with his boss, Gregory, and his loan officer colleagues, Courtney and Thomas. Gregory had long referred to them as the loan officers' group and sometimes the marketing team when he wanted to emphasize that they should be more aggressive in developing loans. Under pressure from Daniel, the bank's new president, he was, in turn, ratcheting up pressure on them. Gregory said the bank was considering changing the bonus formula to be based on group performance, not individual.

Joel had joined Community Bank nearly 20 years ago and watched it become the largest bank on the southwest side of the city. He had heard the mounting talk about teamwork. He was not really against teamwork, certainly it had some appeal for a community bank, but he did not like the bank experimenting with his bonus. He thought tying his bonus to what Courtney and Thomas did was wrong and counterproductive. As the bank leaders had repeated over the years, the bank needs to effectively motivate its salespeople. Community bank has already realized that the best way to motivate salespeople is to give individuals more money the harder they worked and the more business they generated for the bank. The logic is obvious.

True, Joel earned greater bonuses than Courtney and Thomas but that was fair and reasonable. He was their manager and, as the more experienced salesperson, he brought in more business than they did. But Joel had come through the same system, and now it was his turn to benefit. It was not right now that he was the senior salesperson to take away his advantage. Some day Courtney and Thomas would be more productive and more rewarded. The system was fair as well as productive.

Joel's job had already become more difficult lately, as he could not rely heavily on regular customers. Other banks, including national banks, had become more aggressive, entering into Community Bank's natural market without even saying "Hello." Now, on top of this uncertainly, the bank's upper management was adding another burden and distraction of "teamwork."

This was not the first time Gregory had talked about teamwork. Joel had not worried too much about such talk because he knew that Gregory was not prepared to do much more than talk. Joel doubted that Gregory was committed to full-blown teamwork; after all, he developed the current system of rewarding individuals for their individual achievement and had lived under it for years.

But now Daniel was talking more about his vision for the bank as a global local bank, serving the local community at an international standard of excellence. Daniel thought that more teamwork was necessary to realize this vision. He pressured Gregory, and then Gregory pressured the loan officers. But how were they to understand the teamwork concept when the rest of the staff did not?

> "Gregory almost smiled when he asked about the Donaldson deal," Joel told Courtney, a 30-year-old professional with an informal manner and a ready smile who had just recently joined the bank, when he saw her later that morning. "Of course, he's not really asking as much as pressuring us to close the deal."

"Well, Donaldson is one of his old customers," Courtney said. "But times have changed. The Donaldson people have more options and they'll take them."

"Gregory and the people upstairs don't really seem to realize that it's a new world," Joel said. "When we call upon Donaldson, we smile, tell them how happy we are that they're growing and subtly remind them that we have been their go-to bank. But we offer them the same products and services we offered the last time we met. They're smiling less when we leave than when we first got there. That's not good."

"Sounds like our meetings with Gregory," Courtney said. "We're happier when we begin than when we are at the end. That's not a good sign either."

"It's irritating," Joel said. "We hear teamwork talk but the message is still, 'You got to deliver, increase your sales' as though we can do it by ourselves," Joel said.

Thomas came in and joined the conversation. Thomas was born in China but grew up in New York City and had moved across the country to take his current position in the loans office. He was just a year older than Courtney but had been at the bank for three years already. "What do you expect?" he said. "The bosses make the plans, we carry them out."

"This isn't China, Thomas," Joel said. When Thomas arrived at Community Bank, Joel was careful not to offend the newcomer with comments about China. Now he enjoyed teasing him a little.

"That's for sure," Thomas replied. He didn't mind the teasing. "China believes in rapid growth. In getting richer. In getting things done rather than fighting about them."

"Here we're democratic," Joel said. "Everyone can say what's on his mind."

"Really?" Courtney interjected. "What company are you referring to?" As a recent hire, Courtney welcomed these informal conversations, when Joel was more relaxed and open than he was in formal meetings and she could speak up and even have a little fun with him. Speaking up was more difficult when Gregory was in the room.

"Chinese people tend to be more open than Westerners," said Thomas. "Seems like the people in my family, my relatives from China, have a lot of opinions and are willing to express them. They like to complain, especially about the government."

Joel said, "I read something about the virtues of Japanese management."

Thomas saw his chance to give Joel some of his own medicine. "China is not Japan," he said. "Japan is an island, China's a continent. China will soon replace America as the world's largest economy. Think you can get used to that?"

Need for Teamwork Knowledge

Joel was not prepared to understand and accept teamwork at Community Bank. He considered teambuilding irrelevant not only to his own goals and aspirations but also to those of his sales colleagues, indeed, to those of the bank itself. Talk about teamwork at Community Bank seemed just that, talk. He saw few examples of productive teamwork. Top managers, even Daniel and Gregory, did not work well together. He doubted that investing time and energy getting people to work as a team would actually develop teamwork at the bank, and, even if it would, he expected the payoff would be not worth the investment. There were already too many meetings where people tried to get along and got nothing done. Daniel's talk about teamwork left him irritated, not inspired.

However, Daniel talked about the need for more teamwork with growing conviction. He saw positive examples of people working together—and, even more clearly, evidence of the bank's lack of teamwork. His own job and its many frustrations seemed to him to mostly involve trying to undo the effects of ineffective collaboration. After listening and reading about leadership and teamwork in the business press, it now seemed increasingly obvious to him that everyone would be much better off if they more effectively combined their ideas, knowledge, and effort. Everyone would win.

Yet Daniel, Gregory, and other top managers had done little to make teamwork seem attractive and realistic to employees like Joel, Courtney, and Thomas. Upper management talked more about teams but did not lead by example. What's more, they didn't seem to realize that if they weren't committed to the concept and consistent in its application, staff members would continue to focus on their own work and be motivated only to make themselves look good to their superiors.

Bank employees were not hostile to each other, but they did not much feel like teammates either. A few years ago, management considered an annual ranking of employees from first to last, but scarped that idea when employees loudly objected. In current performance appraisals, managers rated their employees relative to others. Only 15 per cent of employees could be rated "outstanding" and at least 10 per cent had to be rated as "needs improvement."

Departments within the bank felt more like rivals than partners, their performances evaluated and compared. Each department had its own suite of offices where members had few opportunities to get to know those in other departments. When issues and frustrations arose, department heads discussed these at management meetings and, when announced to their staff, their responses were not always understood or valued. Departments often felt that they had lost arguments with other departments, especially with the operations department that has the most senior employees.

Not understanding how teamwork functions and how to develop it within the organization were obstacles at Community Bank. For all their talk, Daniel, Gregory, and the rest of top management had only a cursory understanding of the concept, and they didn't appreciate what they needed to do to implement it at the bank.

LEADERSHIP AND ORGANIZATIONS IN TROUBLE

Evidence suggests that many employees around the world believe they have low quality relationships with their leaders and feel unmotivated. In surveys, over 70 per cent of US employees rate their boss as the greatest source of stress on the job (Hogan, Curphy, and Hogan, 1994). Surveys have also found that 23 per cent of US employees would fire their manager and only 18 per cent of the US public rate executives as high or very high on honesty and ethical standards (Kouzes and Posner, 2005). A 2007 Towers Ferrin survey of 900,000 employees worldwide indicated that nearly 40 per cent of the workforce was disenchanted or disengaged from work, in contrast to the just over one fifth of employees who were fully engaged, motivated, and eager to work. The failure to engage employees is costly. Organizations with low employee engagement had a 33 per cent annual decline in earnings growth, whereas organizations where employees were highly engaged had a 19 per cent increase in operating income and a 28 per cent growth in earnings per share. Leading so that employees are engaged and motivated very much adds to the bottom line of companies as well as the wellbeing of leaders and employees.

Appointed as a Manager, but the Need to Act as a Leader

Daniel and Gregory are like the many bright, energetic professionals in companies, and Executive Masters in Business Administration we have worked with over the years. Successful performance earns them promotions to be managers, but this accomplishment often results in frustration for them and their employees.

Through education, training, and experience, professionals have worked to strengthen their own capabilities and motivation. They want to achieve; they enjoy completing concrete tasks and the feeling that they have successfully used their abilities and energy. They see themselves as "self-motivators" who gets things done. The promotion confirms their successful self-development.

After being appointed as a manager, they remain focused on improving their own performance. They assume that they should be the most knowledgeable, hardest-working professional in their group. They should solve major problems, instruct others what to do, and rescue them in crises. But in this process, they are becoming micro-managers who frustrate and stress employees through close supervision.

Rather than completing professional tasks, successful leaders strengthen their followers to get things done. Leaders succeed when their employees succeed. Yet realizing that they should help others be productive is a challenge that many managers do not meet. They never make the transition from being appointed a manager to acting as a leader.

Realizing that managers work with and through others is a first step in making the transition from professional to leader. The second step is to have a clear understanding of the kind of relationships required to work effectively with and through others.

COOPERATIVE RELATIONSHIPS FOR TODAY'S ORGANIZATIONS

Leaders have long been expected to motivate employees so that they are fully engaged in their work and apply themselves to get things done. Traditionally, leaders were thought to be successful by direct influence where they inform employees of their tasks, closely monitor their conformance, and reward desired behavior and sanction undesired behavior.

Today's leaders often have neither the time nor the capability to supervise and direct employees; indeed, employees may work at a distance from their supervisors. Leaders realize that employees themselves should be directed and engaged. Employees are often in a good place to know how they can be effective in their situations. Managers have goals and aspirations for their employees, but these are often only general ideas about what employees should actually do. In today's downsized and geographically spread out organizations, managers' direct monitoring and rewarding specific actions are increasingly ineffective.

Leaders are recognizing that they want to encourage employees to be fully engaged in their work where they feel an internal need to get things done. Managers do not want employees just to comply outwardly with instructions but to be internally committed to accomplishing goals and contributing to the organization. Employees should exercise "self-leadership" where they direct and monitor themselves. They should have "intrinsic motivation" where people feel an internal need to get things done. What should be recognized is that leaders can promote employee engagement through developing quality relationships.

The knowledge that leaders motivate by developing cooperative, open-minded relationships is especially useful for today's leaders. Through cooperative goals and open-minded discussion, leaders convince employees that they not only have valuable goals but they have the support and abilities to reach them. These relationships help employees manage themselves without costly, at times annoying, close monitoring.

Mis-Understanding Leadership as an "I" Thing

Thinking like professionals, Daniel and Gregory assumed that they exercise leadership over Joel and other employees. Indeed, management thinking has long considered leadership as something that some people do to others. The emphasis in practice and in research has been trying to understand what distinguishes individuals so that some are leaders and others are not. Leadership is considered an "I" thing. What are the actions and the underlying personalities of individuals who are successful leaders? What do successful leaders do and why?

For decades managers and researchers have debated these issues and developed a great range of answers. Business leaders like Bill Gates are considered successful because they are driven visionaries; Steve Jobs strengthened Apple by being tough and demanding; Richard Branson developed thriving businesses by caring and supporting people who work for him. It seems that effective leaders have a variety of approaches and personalities. There are no proven scripts for leaders. Leaders must develop their own ways and styles that fit them as well as their employees and organization.

Despite many studies, little progress has been made to identify the personalities and actions that make managers successful leaders. Commands may induce compliance and commitment with one employee, but resentment and resistance with another; an action may be effective in one situation but not another. Research on leadership as an "I" thing has limited practical implications. We cannot expect to understand the effects of leadership personalities and actions separated from the relationships in which they occur.

Understanding Leadership as a "We" Thing

Researchers have concluded that leadership is about relationships. Successful leaders have various strategies and personalities and flexibly use different ways to influence others. What they have in common are interpersonal abilities and sensitivities. Leaders come in great variety with their own personalities and styles, but successful ones develop quality relationships with individual employees within which they influence, are open to influence, and work productively and together. They also develop quality relationships among employees so that employees collaborate effectively with each other as well as with the leader.

With these quality relationships, effective leaders promote employee success and employees help leaders succeed. Through effective team relationships, leaders recognize and encourage employees and teams to feel capable and powerful so that they can combine their abilities to get things done. Leaders do not just do their own thing; leadership is something that leaders and employees do together. Leadership is a "we" thing, not just an "I" thing.

Many studies document that developing quality relationships is a foundation for leaders to help employees be resourceful and productive. The next sections show how leaders who develop strongly cooperative goals and encourage open-minded discussion both with individual employees and among employees are effective motivators. Cooperative relationships help leaders "work with and through others" successfully.

Quality Leader Relationships for Employee Performance

Successful leaders, though they have various styles, are effective to the extent that they develop high quality relationships with their employees (Avolio, Walumbwa, and Weber, 2009; Dulebohn, Bommer, Liden, Brouer, and Ferris, 2012). Leaders tend to develop and maintain relationships with their followers that vary in quality, ranging from in-group to out-group (Graen and Uhl-Bien, 1995; Liden and Graen, 1980). In-group exchange is a high quality relationship characterized by high levels of communication, mutual support, resource sharing, and mutual reliance. In contrast, out-group exchange is a low quality relationship characterized by formal supervision and mistrust with little support and attention.

Leaders with high quality relationships empower followers to perform effectively and find ways to contribute to the organization (Karriker and Williams, 2009; Ozer, 2008). Leaders in the West and in China have more productive employees to the extent that they develop quality relationships with them (Law, Wang, and Hui, 2010; Xu, Huang, Lam, and Miao, 2012).

Studies have clarified the nature of these quality relationships by documenting the value of cooperative teamwork between leaders and employees. Leaders have more productive employees to the extent that they develop cooperative goals and have open-minded discussions with them (Chen and Tjosvold, 2007, 2012; Chen, Liu, and Tjosvold, 2005; Tjosvold, Hui, and Law, 1998; Tjosvold, Poon, and Yu, 2005). Indeed, it has proved very difficult to document situations when leaders have more productive employees by developing competitive relationships with them.

Why should cooperative leader relationships contribute so consistently to effective leadership and performance? With high quality, cooperative relationships, leaders and their employees communicate often and accurately (Abu, Bakar, Dilbeck, and McCroskey, 2010; Kath, Marks, and Ranney, 2010; Lee and Jablin, 1995). Leaders do not rely on one-way instructions and job assignments but discuss tasks and goals directly and fully as they negotiate what needs to be done. With these relationships, employees are prepared to ask questions and express their concerns, provoking leaders to clarify their instructions and plans for them. Employees and leaders are open with their concerns and aspirations as they work to understand each other's needs.

In addition to promoting two-way communication and understanding, cooperative relationships help employees appreciate the importance and value of assignments. As they discuss, leaders show and explain so that employees realize how their work contributes to the efforts of others and promote the organization as a whole. Employees are not just asked to be busy and do things but realize how their efforts and success are contributing to important team and organizational goals. Employees are more motivated when they find their tasks meaningful.

Cooperative, open-minded relationships also help convince employees that they will have sufficient resources and information to accomplish challenging tasks. Their open dialogue helps leaders and employees have a clear understanding of the resources needed to accomplish tasks. Together they identify the obstacles employees confront and how they can together overcome them. Their discussion helps leaders and employees know the assistance and resources needed to accomplish the tasks and believe that these resources will be forthcoming. Employees who have quality relationships with their leaders are more confident that they can together deal with unanticipated barriers.

Leaders cannot expect employees to work hard and effectively if they do not believe that they have a practical path and necessary resources to achieve. Through cooperative relationships and dialogue, leaders and employees integrate their ideas to develop tasks, time tables, and resources for effective performance. Then employees are convinced that they have the capacity to succeed and become committed to accomplish their meaningful tasks.

Cooperative Team Relationships for Motivation

Researchers now emphasize that successful leaders promote quality relationships among employees as well as between themselves and employees. Leaders are effective to the extent that they develop cooperative relationships among employees. For example, Wong and Tjosvold (2010) observed that cooperative relationships among project team members led them to believe that their group was powerful and potent; this confidence in turn led the team to be productive. However, with low quality, competitive relationships, team members did not expect mutual help, felt powerless, and were unproductive.

Like those between leader and employees, cooperative relationships among employees can convince them that they can get their tasks completed and contribute to the team and organization. In searching for whether work goals can be reached, employees want to know the extent that their colleagues will help them. Employees typically need each other's information and assistance to get things done. If others will not help them, employees are more pessimistic that they can succeed. With high quality relationships though, employees very much expect that their colleagues will provide concrete assistance as well as general encouragement. Quality relationships among employees convince employees that they will receive each other's assistance and resources so that they can accomplish their goals.

Leaders have long been told that having employees and departments competing with each other motivates them, much like having companies competing for customers in the marketplace. People will work hard to be better than others. From this viewpoint, strong leaders foster competition, resulting in superior performance as people do their best to outdo each other.

However, as discussed in Chapter 2, summaries of hundreds of studies document that cooperative relationships motivate people to perform compared to those working competitively or independently (Johnson and Johnson, 2005). These results are strong and consistent: The effects of cooperation compared to competition on performance are practically as well as statistically significant and occur in many situations, including both between and within groups. Cooperative relationships are more productive than competitive relationships in many situations.

Leaders, though, can be flexible in that competition can at times motivate and be useful. For example, having individuals see who is the best bowler or has the funniest joke can be exciting and a welcomed break from the routine. However, promoting competition typically undermines motivation and performance, especially for challenging tasks. For most important situations, developing cooperative relationships among employees helps them and their leaders succeed.

VARIOUS LEADERSHIP STYLES EFFECTIVE THROUGH COOPERATIVE TEAMWORK

Researchers are recognizing that various leadership styles are effective to the extent that they develop quality relationships among employees (Xu and Thomas, 2011). Transformational leaders were found effective not by unilaterally directing employees and commanding change but by helping employees manage their conflicts with each other cooperatively and thereby coordinate their efforts constructively (Zhang, Cao, and Tjosvold, 2011). Government officials who exercised transformational leadership promoted cooperative conflict management that, in turn, resulted in strong government–business partnerships (Wong, Wei, and Tjosvold, 2014). Productive and people-oriented leaders in India strengthened their teams by fostering open-minded discussion among team members (Bhatnagar and Tjosvold, 2012). Servant leaders emphasize service to others, team consensus, and personal development. They were found effective to the extent that they foster open-minded teamwork. By developing teams that manage their conflicts cooperatively and open-mindedly, servant leaders help employees coordinate their work and deliver quality customer service (Wong, Liu, and Tjosvold, 2014). When considered together, these results indicate that leaders, whether they have charismatic or servant leadership styles, are effective to the extent that they develop cooperative, open-minded relationships among their followers.

Conclusions

This chapter describes how cooperative team relationships very much help leaders "work with and through others." These cooperative relationships are central to fulfilling leaders' traditional role of motivating employees to perform effectively. Cooperative relationships help leaders and employees understand each other's interests, develop meaningful work goals, and identify the ways and resources needed to accomplish these goals and overcome obstacles. High quality cooperative relationships motivate because they develop mutual commitment to each other's success.

Chapter 6 shows how leaders and employees can strengthen cooperative goals that underline high quality relationships. Chapter 7 describes how these relationships help leaders and teams discuss issues and views openmindedly and constructively.

Action Plans

Do less of:

- Work as a specialist rather than a leader.
- Exert leadership unilaterally on employees.
- Develop leadership skills by yourself.
- Closely monitor employees to ensure performance.
- Attribute poor customer service to the salesperson.

Do more of:

- Lead as a "we" thing, not an "I" thing.
- Focus on developing quality relationships with and among employees.
- Work through teams to get things done.
- Use your leadership style to develop open-minded cooperative teams.
- Motivate employees by promoting cooperative relationships that encourage mutual support and assistance.
- Develop cooperative, open-minded relationships so that teams can solve issues and manage themselves.

6

Strengthen Cooperative Goals

We cannot live only for ourselves. A thousand fibers connect us with our fellow-men; and along those fibers, as sympathetic threads our actions run as causes, and they come back to us as effects.

Herman Melville

A year ago, Daniel was thankful and honored that the board had appointed him president of Community Bank. He knew that the bank could continue to make important contributions to his city and his old neighborhood. But he also knew the bank would have to change and that he would need to lead so that it did change.

During his Executive Masters of Business Administration (EMBA) studies, there was much talk about how leaders manage change. He felt the EMBA experience, especially with the strong relationships and ongoing discussion with other managers, had helped him become more of a leader. He really believed that leaders work with and through others: Leaders do not simply do their own jobs but help others succeed.

Now, though, he did not feel so well prepared for his new position, especially the managing change part. That the bank needed to change was clear. Its markets had new customers with different needs as well as new suppliers with different capabilities. When he talked about the need to change, everyone nodded in agreement. But change to what and how were not very clear or much embraced.

As an employee and manager, he had endured a number of fads and fashions as his previous bank tried to manage change. But these efforts did not pay off much. He had concluded: Changes in structures and procedures could make things better but they also could make things worse; for sure, though, these changes required time, effort, and expense. Change initiatives can distract as well as focus.

Contrary to his hope, becoming president did not clarify how he could strengthen Community Bank. Trying to find effective ways to change, he read and attended talks and conferences. He wanted to be confident that the changes he proposed would be wise investments where the payoff would be much more than the costs. He followed a basic rule of good management: "Don't make things worse."

He readily believed writers who espoused the value of strengthening teamwork. Surely, the bank and everyone working there would be better off if people shared their ideas and resources willingly and effectively. Everyone would win. When he read that researchers had shown that leaders can have a particularly positive impact by improving teamwork he willingly accepted the idea and began to think that this would be a way to manage change at the bank. But how could he improve teamwork? Indeed, what is effective teamwork? What could he do to bring it about?

Although scheduling more morning meetings was not attractive, he was happy that he had joined the "Leadership Development Team," (LDT). Leslie Graham, an instructor at the local college who had established the group, explained that LDT was like a book club. Leaders from various local business and non-profit organizations would read and discuss management articles and books. They would help each other understand ideas and plan how to apply them. They would learn leadership together so that they could then help their organizations change.

Daniel was so inspired by these early meetings that he had begun to talk about the need for more teamwork at Community Bank. When probed about what he meant and what he planned to do, he mentioned that the bank should experiment with team bonuses. The bank would reward teams to the extent that they accomplish their goals. Then bank employees would see that by helping each other, discussing their ideas openly, and providing each other with resources, they themselves would be rewarded.

Team bonuses seemed like a powerful way to get people to think "we." Daniel thought that team bonuses communicated what he meant about teamwork and were a concrete way of developing it. He had not anticipated the confusion, questions, and anxiety that his proposal had generated.

However, he received good feedback when he talked about his efforts at Community Bank at the morning's LDT meeting. His LDT teammates congratulated him at taking the first steps and endorsed his idea to have the lecturer conduct an experience on solving problems as a team. Daniel argued that this experience should remind bank managers and employees that working as a team is very practical; it's not unusual or unrealistic. Working as a team is a fundamental way that people have always got things done.

LDT teammates emphasized that he should welcome Community Bank employees' questions and comments and show that he was listening to them. Daniel should reassure bank employees that he would not impose change but that they were going to change as a team. He wanted all employees to understand the nature of teamwork so that they could work as partners to develop it.

With this support and the help of the lecturer, Daniel felt that he could develop an afternoon workshop to help his colleagues consider becoming a team organization. They would better understand teamwork and what they would need to do to work as a team. They would begin to see that investments in teamwork could payoff for them and the bank.

"Wasn't so bad, was it?" Thomas teased Joel as they met in their common office area the day after bank employees had a half a day teambuilding retreat with a team exercise. "I think you were really into solving that murder mystery. I'm glad you did not bang the table too loudly in your excitement."

"Okay, it was not as bad as I feared," Joel said. "But we're not a detective agency, we're a bank pushing loans."

"But we had good results solving the problem when we worked as a team," Courtney said.

"It was set up that way," Joel said. "Each person received different clues and to use all the clues people had to tell us what was on their cards. How often does that happen?"

"Often," Thomas said. "Some people may know more than others, but usually others have some information and ideas that can help solve the problem."

"Why not just pick the person who knows and let her do it?" Joel countered.

"Yes, but you have to know who that person is," Courtney said. "In our case, it wouldn't always be Gregory." She had often heard Joel complain that though Gregory is the boss, he doesn't always know best.

"I'll drink to that," Joel said. "However, when one person has all the relevant knowledge, all the clues to solve the murder mystery, then he or she should do it alone."

"But it's more than just knowing things," Thomas said. "We had to organize all the clues and put them together to rule out certain suspects and to be sure we had the culprit, the motive, and the weapon. It was challenging too, but not so stressful as we're all talking."

"I got involved," Joel conceded. "Fun to let off steam. You have to admit this was just a fun problem. When problems are difficult, then there would be more frustrations."

"Seems to me we need teamwork more for those problems," Thomas said. "When the going gets tough, the team gets going, as Daniel said."

"I don't want to sound too old," Joel said. "But I've heard too many speeches by management gurus."

Courtney welcomed change at the bank, especially change that would help her cope with the stress of developing new customers. She felt if she could work more with Joel and Thomas, her work and life at the bank would be much less burdensome and more productive. She enjoyed the give and take of discussion, getting to know Joel and Thomas better, and feeling more connected to the bank.

Courtney found Daniel convincing. She believed him when he talked about how they would all be better off as individuals and as a bank if they solved problems and got things done together. Perhaps the message was not brand new but she believed.

Joel was not ready to be convinced even if Courtney was. He did not want to be misled by another fancy sounding slogan that wasted his time.

Thomas agreed with Courtney that Daniel was committed, arguing that he even had his own team.

"I give him credit," Joel said. "He was candid about meeting regularly with other CEOs to discuss books and learn more about leadership and teamwork."

"It's good," Courtney agreed. "He's leading by example; if we should learn, he should learn first. He is serious about developing his leadership."

Joel agreed that Daniel was walking the walk as well as talking the talk.

"I like his point on helping us develop our relationships," Thomas said. "My relatives are always talking about how important relationships are in China to get anything done."

"We're moving to China, did the president say that too," Joel joked.

"But relationships are important in the US too," Thomas said.

"None of us had a serious interest in solving the murder mystery," Joel said. "Who cares? But in our work, we have quotas to meet, performance appraisals to endure, bonuses to earn."

"True," Thomas said. "We need to see that this teamwork will pay off in the real world of banking."

"We need more convincing that this teamwork program will be worth the effort," Joel said.

"Interesting that Daniel said that we're going to work as a team to become a team," Courtney said.

"Well, it sounds catchy, we will see what it actually means," Joel said. "He's off to a rocky start in my mind with his team incentives."

"What's up with that?" Thomas said.

Daniel thought that a question and answer session could respond to concerns bank employees had about team bonuses and to move the team-work program ahead. They would discuss together as a team to clarify what it means to work as a team: The method reinforced the message.

The LDT team had reminded him that it's the questions and complaints left unanswered that can really obstruct his developing teamwork plans. He asked Leslie to join the session to serve as a resource about teamwork knowledge. Daniel would lead the session.

Daniel welcomed employees and reminded them that the purpose of the session was to discuss team bonuses and teamwork more generally. He asked them to turn to the person sitting next to them and find out each other's ideas, questions, and concerns about team bonuses and teamwork.

Stephen from the financial management area began the question period. He doubted that team bonuses were effective or fair. People were concerned for their own interests; we cannot expect them to be altruistic. Companies recognize this and have begun to pay for performance, that is, when individuals do well, they make more money. People who don't perform well should be held accountable, not other people.

Daniel explained that with a team bonus, people get paid for performance. The better the team performs, the bigger the bonus to distribute among the team members.

Stephen objected that they would be denied a bonus if team members did not perform. He felt people would be penalized for others' failures and that team bonuses are unfair. Daniel said that he recognized that others also had similar concerns. Although people decide themselves and teams cannot force members to perform, team members can, though, help each other to do well. In a strong team with a group bonus, team members want each other to do well so that the group performs and each of them is rewarded.

Christina, Stephen's colleague in finance, followed up. As they had studied in economics, people engage in social loafing and free riding where people just let others do the work. When everyone is responsible, no one feels responsible and people loaf. Having their own assignment means that people know they cannot just let others do the job.

Daniel was surprised at the strength of the apprehensions about team bonuses. But he enjoyed the give and take and it was good to respond to employee concerns. He also knew that he did not have to answer all the questions quickly. He wanted people to get involved and discuss.

> "It does not have to be that way," Donna from the market research group said. "Having teammates counting on you to do your part can pressure us to perform. It can be easier to say 'No' to your boss than to a teammate.
>
> Of course I personally would never say 'No' to Gregory." Donna liked to make people laugh as much as she liked to make points. "I can see where other people in other companies sometimes ignore their boss. I especially see it in the movies."
>
> "I also see that in the movies and elsewhere too," Gregory joined in the fun.
>
> "Good discussion," Daniel said. "Teams need individuals to do their part, but teammates are in a good position to help, encourage, and hold each person accountable."
>
> Christina then asked, "What do the managers do then if employees are to help and hold each other accountable for doing their own tasks?"
>
> "Another good question," Daniel said. "We managers should help you work together. That's why we want more workshops and seminars on teamwork. We managers should help departments work together. That is what I was trying to do with team bonuses."
>
> "I thought this teamwork was to make us more cooperative with each other," Thomas said. "But now it sounds like we have to be tough with

each other, demand each other perform. Sounds rough, seems not very cooperative to me."

"You're right, working together is a lot tougher than it sounds," Daniel said.

Leslie added that she had found in her work trying to help others work together that leaders and employees should have a clear understanding of cooperation. Cooperation is when people's goals go together. As one succeeds, others succeed. It is definitely not the opposite of conflict. Conflict occurs when people's actions interfere, like when one team member does not complete his or her task on time. So when people cooperate, they also disagree and have other conflict.

"But people have the same goals when they cooperate, why would they disagree," Christina argued.

"They disagree about the best way to reach their goals, over who should do what where, when they will know they have reached their goals, how they should treat each other, all sorts of things," Leslie replied.

"People working together as a team can have conflict," Donna agreed.

"Sometimes a lot of conflict," Leslie said. "But cooperative teams are in a good position to manage conflict because they try to resolve the conflict so that everyone can reach their goals."

"I always thought that it was when people competed, that they had conflict," Stephen said. "They are fighting over who can do things better, who has the best ideas. That is why competition is productive."

"Competition is when people's goals are against each other; if one wins, the other loses; if one is right, the other is wrong," Leslie said. "So conflict is also built into competition."

"Seems like there is no getting away from this conflict," Thomas said.

"That's right, we have a choice about whether we believe our goals are cooperative or competitive but we're going to have conflict either way," Leslie said. "We can't opt out of conflict. But we can strengthen our cooperative goals."

"I can see where we can benefit from more reading and discussion about cooperation, competition, and conflict," Daniel said. "We need more than team bonuses."

"Why are we neglecting competition?" Stephen asked. "Competition works for the economy, it should work for us."

Leslie explained that researchers have not been able to document many situations in organizations when competition is more constructive than cooperation. We all know that competition can be good, fun sometimes too. Many people enjoy contests and sports. However, statistical summaries of research studies indicate that for most situations for most objectives, cooperation is superior. In most situations, cooperation gets the job done, reinforces relationships, helps manage stress, and even strengthens self-confidence.

"How can that be?" Christina disagreed. "Winning develops character and confidence."

"Researchers were surprised too, but the finding that competition is not a good basis for self-confidence is quite strong," Leslie said. "Remember that in working as a team, people get a lot of positive feedback and appreciation as they help each other succeed. In competition, you have to celebrate by yourself. You might win today, but will you win tomorrow? You don't know."

"Not so easy to understand or to believe," Christina said.

"No rush," Daniel said. "We can read and discuss more, understand more."

"We should have more studying and discussing," Leslie said. "As I think you will see, cooperation can give a lot of value to people and organizations."

"Cooperation has to be practical," Stephen said. "But it does not seem easy to develop cooperative goals. Even with a team bonus people may not feel cooperative."

Leslie argued that teams can and should strengthen cooperative goals continually. She promised to send readings on ways that teams can develop cooperative goals. Perhaps the bank could have a workshop where teams together create ways to convince everyone on the team that their goals are cooperative, that as one team member succeeds, others succeed.

"I guess this is what you mean when you say we should invest in team-work," Stephen said.

"Teams have to keep strengthening cooperative goals, or else they get weaker," Leslie said.

"This discussion has brought home to me that we need much more than team bonuses to develop cooperative teamwork," Daniel concluded.

"It won't be so bad," Donna said. "We can do it together."

How to Strengthen Cooperative Goals

Daniel's discussions about cooperation and team bonuses had elicited interest but also anxieties. What did he mean exactly and what would they be asked to do? Would the effort to develop cooperative teamwork actually pay off?

Daniel and others at Community Bank began to realize that they needed precise discussions where they agree on the meaning of key terms. Otherwise, they risked deep confusion when people use the same word to mean different things.

Cooperation, competition, and conflict are especially prone to having various meanings that can add a great deal of confusion to discussions and making plans. Fortunately, Community Bank employees could read and learn from books, articles, and studies on cooperation and competition and develop a common understanding of the nature of cooperation so that they could work together toward a team organization.

Daniel and bank employees were also realizing that they should "walk the talk" as well as "talk the talk." They needed to follow discussion with experimenting using ideas to strengthen Community Bank. They would learn more about cooperation as they tried to develop cooperative goals where teammates believe that they "swim or sink" together. Their goals reinforce each other so that one person's success helps others succeed.

Developing strong cooperative goals is challenging. Deep suspicions in organizations, high divorce rates in families, enduring ethnic tensions in societies, and hot and cold wars reflect this challenge. Even apparently stable relationships fragment; friends become enemies. Fortunately, enemies can become friends.

Strengthening cooperative goals requires an ongoing effort to provide a solid foundation for productive teamwork. Individuals bring powerful achievement, affiliation, identity, and other needs to the workplace. Cooperative relationships channel the energy of these motives into productive work for organizations and people. However, these motives can be expressed competitively and independently, very much undermining relationships and openness. While team members can decide that their goals are cooperative, they can also decide that their goals are competitive and independent.

This section describes evidence that can convince team members that their goals are cooperative. The stronger and more overlapping the evidence, the more likely it is that teammates will believe that their important goals are cooperative.

Develop Team Tasks

Joel had long thought that he had his own individual task of developing profitable loans. But he had realized over the years that involving department members in this task could be useful. Customers seemed to enjoy and be reassured when Thomas and Courtney joined company visits. Discussions among the three of them after company visits could release tension and help develop follow-ups. Joel appreciated talking with Thomas and Courtney about how to approach customers and brainstorming how the bank could best serve them. The idea of assigning the tasks of developing the loans to the team did not seem strange, though team rewards still seemed like a big step to him.

Accomplishing tasks is necessary for organizations but it also helps individuals meet their achievement needs to perform effectively as well as serve other requirements and values. Structuring group tasks help forge powerful individual motives into cooperative work: Teammates conclude that by helping the group get its jobs done, they can feel they have performed well and contributed to teammates and to the organization.

Leaders ask the team as whole to accomplish a task. The team should make one set of recommendations, develop and produce a new product, or solve a problem. Team members are to integrate their ideas and develop one solution. Each team member signs off on the team's output, indicating that he or she has contributed and supports it.

The team regularly measures its productivity. Team members consider feedback and records so that they keep informed of progress and what is necessary for completion. Factory workers, call center employees, and others who work primarily on individual tasks can combine their individual output to form a group average each week. They commit themselves to improving others' as well as their own output.

Tasks should be challenging to make it easier for team members to recognize that they cannot succeed working individually but need the combined consideration, thinking, and effort of all team members to do so. For example, the team is expected to develop a marketing plan acceptable to sales personnel; to make it more challenging, they help the sales personnel learn how to develop their own plans in the future.

Challenging tasks that are probable but difficult to achieve have been found to engage achievement needs. Then members can demonstrate that they have accomplished a task at a high level and have the internal feeling of being effective.

Team members develop tasks that may not be apparent to managers but are very useful for the organization. Team members brainstorm possible tasks that can further the organization as well as their individual aspirations. They negotiate until they decide on tasks that promote to the extent possible both the interests of the organization and team members.

Learning and improvement tasks are particularly constructive. All group members are expected to improve their technical and team skills; these skills can be operating machinery, selling products, and managing people. Each employee is responsible for keeping his or her own output up; they can make the task more challenging and cooperative by adding that they should help each other improve their individual performance. Team members give each other feedback, model effective ways to work, and encourage experimenting to help each other learn and improve their individual performance.

Assign Roles to Divide the Work

Christina thought that teamwork leads to social loafing where, as everyone is responsible for getting things done, no one is responsible. But cooperative teamwork occurs when team members coordinate their individual work. A team member focuses on one aspect of the team task and completes it, knowing that teammates will complete others.

Managers and team members should develop roles for individuals. Roles identify the major activities and tasks for the group to succeed and then distribute them to individuals and sub-groups; everyone knows what he or she should get done and how it complements the work of others.

Roles can help team members participate effectively. One member is asked to record ideas, another to encourage full participation, another to be a devil's advocate to challenge common views, and a fourth observes and provides feedback to help the group reflect on its workings.

Cooperative goals and division of labor are essential for developing expertise. Team members encourage each other to develop and apply their abilities so that they can all succeed. As there is no need to replicate others' work, individuals can specialize by developing specific knowledge and expertise and applying them to their part of the common task. Without cooperative goals and a division of labor, team members are tempted to believe they have to do every step themselves.

Roles formalize the division of labor that is a central element of organizations. Organizations assign individuals and departments different tasks and functions so that the organization as a whole accomplishes its goals. Organizations are perhaps our most useful social invention in large part because of cooperative goals and division of labor. Pharmaceutical companies combine the expertise and work of clinical physicians, chemists, biologists, and statisticians to form a new product team tasked with developing and testing new drugs.

Although roles are very useful, individuals and departments can be so focused on their part of the work that they neglect, even reject coordinating with others in the organization. To be effective roles and division of labor must be complemented with coordination. In addition to recognizing that each member has a role that needs to be performed for the team to function, team members should also realize how their role performances will be coordinated. Each team member performs his or her own role but is not just doing his or her own thing.

Team members should recognize and clarify how their roles are complementary. The team leader, assistant leader, researcher, and secretary discuss how their responsibilities supplement each other so that they recognize no one can be highly effective unless others do their jobs. In cross functional teams, marketing, production, and other specialists let each other know their specialized knowledge and how they plan to apply it; teammates then discuss how they will combine their knowledge and effort.

Use Everyone's Abilities

A common stereotype of cooperation is that it depends upon abundant resources: When resources are scare, we compete. But scarce resources are an important reason for cooperation. People recognize that they need each other's abilities to be successful; no one person can accomplish the task alone. When each team member has only a portion of the information, skills, and other resources necessary to accomplish the task, they recognize that they need each other to contribute and pool their resources. Abundant resources may tempt some people to try to be a hero and show that they are better than others.

Team members should identify their own individual abilities and talents so that they appreciate how each one can move the group toward goal attainment. A new product team recognizes that it must blend the skills of the marketing, engineering, research, and manufacturing specialists to produce a viable commercial product.

Teams can deliberately distribute resources so that each team member is given a part of what is necessary to get the job done. For example, each member of a team is asked to study material on different aspects of working as a team; one studies cooperative goals, another competitive and independent goals, a third open-mindedness, and a fourth leadership. Then they come together to make sure they all understand these aspects of teamwork and how they fit together.

Joel, Courtney, and Thomas share an open space with their desks close to each other; they can easily meet informally to discuss common issues and feel more like a team. Ad hoc exchanges can create unexpected insights. The physical closeness of people, that is density, can be very useful, as one author has experienced living in Hong Kong!

Reward Individuals Based on Group Performance

Shared rewards means that if the team succeeds, then each member will receive tangible and intangible benefits. Team members understand that their own individual rewards depend upon team progress. Either everyone is rewarded or no one is rewarded. For unsuccessful teams, individuals are not rewarded and may even suffer consequences.

There are a number of ways to reward individuals based on group performance. Each team member receives a monetary bonus based on the team's success. A sales team has a night on the town for achieving more than expected. Members of a new product team might receive 5 per cent of the profits for a new product that is distributed to team members.

Intangible rewards can be very powerful. Leaders meet team members to appreciate and recognize the team's success. The company newsletter describes the team's accomplishments and contributions. The team throws a party to show that they appreciate each other.

Unequal rewards have the risk that they induce a feeling of rivalry over who should get the most benefits. However, unequal rewards accepted as fair and reasonable promote unity. Although the task force leader is given 5 per cent of the cost savings from the first year's use of a new inventory system, each member accepts 3 per cent as reasonable for them because the task force leader contributed much more effort. Equal rewards do not necessarily mean identical rewards, but rather that rewards are fair and unbiased.

Team rewards should be emphasized but an unproductive group should be held accountable. Humiliation of course is seldom useful. However, leaders should confront unproductive teams. Leaders and team members should avoid the temptation to blame a few, but hold the group as a whole responsible.

Daniel thought that proposing team bonuses would communicate both that he was serious about strengthening teamwork and what he meant by cooperation: When the team does well, everyone gets rewarded, therefore, everyone should contribute. But the team rewards proposal raised concerns as well. Joel and many employees began to worry that they would be blamed because others are irresponsible. They may remember school group projects where they had to step in and work all night before the assignment was due to avoid failing the assignment. Others worried that their teammates would make their work more difficult: They may remember group projects where an arrogant teammate insisted on his way and they could only withdraw and let him do it his way. Through more discussion and during the questions and answers period, Daniel and other employees came to realize that team rewards had to be supplemented with other evidence of cooperative goals as well as the skills to work together.

Build a Community

Team tasks and rewards are hard evidence of cooperative goals but team members do more than mechanically calculate to decide with whom that they "are in this together." Social psychologists have found that people turn to others to understand who they are and how capable they are. The confidence and foundation of the individual depends upon the status and value of the groups he belongs to. The more esteemed one's family, work groups, and ethnic national groups, the stronger the individual.

Team members ask questions such as: Are the people in this team those they want to be with and identify with? Will belonging to this team reinforce their own beliefs of the kind of person they are? Will the groups they already identify with think more highly of them if they wholeheartedly join this team? Answering these questions with "yes" strengthens cooperative goals.

Knowing team members as individuals builds feelings that they can count on each other whereas they are leery of team members they do not know. Team members can discuss their experiences, feelings, and values and engage in "small talk" about family and oneself to strengthen personal relationships. Expressing warmth, friendliness, and concern further helps team members believe that they will feel accepted, valued, and supported. Social gatherings such as Friday afternoon social hours, reward celebrations, and holiday parties encourage feelings of unity.

Team members can show they care about individual teammates by responding to their special needs, celebrating their personal victories, and supporting them in times of crisis. Ideally, this caring culture can also be demonstrated to people who are in need. At our family business, employees work together to raise funds to build and support a primary school in Cameroon, send toys and other supplies to children in refugee camps in Thailand, help find homes for refugee dogs, and feed the homeless in the local community.

Team members feel united when they share a common identity and believe they belong to one community. They choose a name and motto that describes their personalities and their team projects. Teams develop their own value statement. These values emphasize that they belong together and should be helpful "citizens" to each other. They recall stories and examples that illustrate the vision, values, and unity of the team.

As discussed in Chapter 4, norms are typically rules regarding how team members should treat each other. Team members discuss their present norms and decide the norms they want that will enhance them as individuals and strengthen themselves as a team and promote their work. Team members then know what to expect and need less monitoring and influencing. Making norms public and understanding how to follow them is useful to strengthen coordination and unity feelings.

Team tasks, roles to divide the work, utilizing each member's abilities, and developing a community are powerful evidence that team members' goals are cooperatively related. Leaders and members can apply this knowledge in practical and powerful ways to strengthen their teamwork. However, team members themselves must use this evidence to decide that they really do "swim or sink" together.

Choosing Cooperative Goals as a Team

Deciding to cooperate with others can be very challenging. You may believe that there is strong evidence that your goals are cooperatively related to your teammates. However, to work together cooperatively and productively requires your teammates also to choose cooperation. We realize that we cannot cooperate by ourselves. We do not want to look foolish and leave ourselves vulnerable by working cooperatively when others are poised to take advantage of us. Although individuals can compete by themselves, cooperation requires two and sometimes many people to choose to work together.

Team leaders and members should coordinate decisions so that it is clear everyone is concluding that their goals are cooperative. It is important to study this and other books to make sure each person understands cooperative goals and working open-mindedly. Then they should discuss how cooperative teamwork would benefit themselves as individuals and their team performance. The need for everyone to commit to cooperative teamwork and then develop a common plan about how to strengthen their cooperative teamwork should be discussed.

Team members can begin meetings by openly declaring that they will cooperate and work together. They should specify to the team how they will help each other reach their goals and the team succeed. Team members then reciprocate each other's assistance to implement these pledges.

Choosing cooperation should be ongoing. New team members join, new demands are made, and new barriers and opportunities are encountered. These developments may challenge members and tempt them to conclude that their goals are no longer cooperative, but competitive and independent. Team members continually appreciate that they have team tasks, complementary roles and resources, and community feelings and they celebrate that they feel united.

The golden problem of cooperation is: Who will be the first person to commit to working cooperatively? Who will be the first to show that he or she believes that they can rely upon others as they have the capabilities and motivation to help each other reach their goals?

To deal with the golden problem, our advice is to begin with you and go first. Sometimes you have to show a second time, and even more often, that you are convinced that goals are cooperative and you want to work openly with each other so that everyone succeeds. Although taking these steps may be risky, they can pay off in long-term rewarding collaboration and avoiding the costs of prolonged competition with teammates.

Need for Ongoing Development

Research has documented that cooperative goals are a strong foundation for team discussion, coordination, and productivity. Leaders and team members have several central ways that they can strengthen their cooperative goals so that they can confidently feel that they are in this together and are on the same side. They can then recognize that it is to each person's self interest to help other team members succeed.

Building cooperative goals is a concrete way to strengthen trust between team members. Trust is a complex idea but at its heart is the belief that we can rely on others. Cooperative goals make trust reasonable and rational. With cooperative goals, team members expect others to promote their goals because, by doing so, they also promote their own goals. In contrast, competitive and independent goals do not provide a basis for expecting help from others; indeed, they are realistic reasons for suspicion.

This chapter identified major ways to strengthen cooperative goals, but there are many ways that cooperative goals can weaken as well as strengthen. Team members can focus on their individual rather than group tasks; they can understand their role as fulfilling their own responsibilities rather than being part of a team effort; they can focus on developing and using their own abilities rather than everyone's; they can seek rewards of outdoing others rather than sharing group rewards; and they can focus only on their own wellbeing rather than the community's. Leaders and team members must then confront these fragmenting elements as well as continually strengthen cooperative goals.

Action Plans

Do less of:

- Announce and sell that goals are cooperative.
- Talk about cooperation, then recognize individuals for being better than others.
- Assume others should always take the first steps to work cooperatively.

Do more of:

- Recognize that making cooperation constructive is challenging and that making competition constructive is much more challenging.
- Appreciate that employee beliefs about how their goals are related drive their interaction.
- Provide multiple reasons and evidence so that team members are convinced their goals are cooperative.
- Build community feelings where team members know and value each other as individuals.
- Develop team tasks and ask for a solution that integrates the best ideas of all team members.
- Assign complementary roles to divide the work and to understand how teammates should coordinate their efforts.
- Take the first steps to declare and act cooperatively.
- Have teammates publically announce that they will work cooperatively.
- Reward individuals as their team succeeds.

chapter 7

Working Open-Mindedly

Have you learned lessons only of those who admired you,
and were tender with you, and stood aside for you?

Have you not learned great lessons from those who braced
themselves against you, and disputed the passage with you?
                                                    Walt Whitman

Daniel and his Leader Development Team (LTD) members liked the idea that they should develop teamwork by working with employees as a team. They could show what teamwork looked like as they introduced and developed more teamwork in their organizations. Imposing teamwork directly would be ineffective; it sent the wrong message that the leader alone drives teamwork. Team members themselves must make their teams work. The method of change should reinforce the message of teamwork.

Research on cooperation and competition gave them a clear understanding of the underlying relationships that promote productive teamwork. They could describe and help team members develop cooperative relationships as the foundation for teamwork. But team members must actually work together to realize the benefits of these relationships.

The more Daniel's LTD members read and discussed, the more they appreciated the demands of teamwork. Team members must confront and make decisions about how they should proceed to complete their tasks and resolve issues and roadblocks so that they continue to coordinate. With different habits of working and standards, team members have conflicts about when they should meet and how long the meetings should last. Some people prefer emails where others want to talk on the phone. How can they make sure everyone speaks up and contributes? How should they arrange their offices?

No wonder teamwork is often discussed, less often implemented. Teamwork sounds good but the closer one comes to it the more one recognizes the challenges of working together. There are very significant rewards certainly for working as a team, but its demands are considerable and come first. They agreed with Leslie that teamwork is not free, it takes investment.

The LDT members recognized that leaders are tempted to try to resolve issues and solve problems for teams. However, having superiors make and impose decisions on teams should be the exception. Teams must manage themselves to be effective. With many decisions to make, and sometimes very quickly, it is impractical to have an organizational superior make them. In addition, organizational superiors often do not have the knowledge, expertise, and perspective to make effective decisions about how the team should work together. Teams must be able to make many of their own decisions to coordinate and get things done.

Leslie reiterated that leaders are powerful and effective when they help team members make decisions. Strengthening cooperative relationships is the foundation but leaders should also help team members work together productively.

But what should leaders tell teams about how they should work together? LDT members brainstormed ways that team members should discuss issues and work together. They concluded that teammates should share their knowledge, assist each other, swap ideas, and engage in dialogue about issues. They can be effective through giving advice to each other, exchanging their resources, and helping the team feel empowered. Team members interact in many ways depending on their tasks and the situation.

Leslie argued that open-minded discussion is a powerful way to understand how team members should work together as they make decisions and manage themselves. Studies have shown that when team members discuss their various ideas directly with each other, they become curious and work to understand the other's arguments. Then they are in a good position to combine the best of everyone's ideas into an effective decision that team members understand and are committed to.

This openness sounded good to the LDT members; indeed, they hoped for these kinds of discussions for their board and management groups. But if having open-minded discussions is difficult at top management levels, how can they reasonably expect young, less experienced, and less educated employees to do so?

Leslie said that studies have shown not only that managers and executives can discuss issues open-mindedly and productively, but that middle managers and workers on the shop floor can too. Studies also document that open-mindedness helps develop strong relationships with customers and between leaders and employees.

LDT members appreciated this knowledge but they also had questions. These discussions seemed to be the exception in that they contained many more listless conversations with an occasional heated argument about who is right and who is wrong. How can these open-minded discussions be encouraged?

Leslie argued that cooperative goals are the basis for open-mindedness. Teammates with cooperative relationships are willing to express their ideas and consider and combine the ideas of others so that to the extent possible they all benefit. Those with competitive relationships often avoid controversy; if they do disagree openly, they resist combining their ideas and try to have their ideas dominate.

How can leaders help employees understand open-mindedness and strengthen their skills? After a lengthy discussion, LTD members concluded that just describing open-mindedness to employees would risk sounding too abstract and idealistic. Employees may dismiss such discussion as wishful thinking rather than an approach they can use to resolve issues and manage themselves.

Their readings had introduced the procedure of advocacy teams where people are assigned opposing views and then practice open-minded discussion. First they prepare to disagree, then they disagree directly, next they demonstrate they understand the opposing arguments by restating them, and finally they drop their assigned positions to combine the best ideas to create solutions that are mutually beneficial.

Daniel wondered whether they could use advocacy teams with the employees so that they experience and practice open-mindedness. Perhaps they could discuss the pros and cons of team bonuses and teamwork.

LDT members were intrigued but also skeptical. Would employees be willing to get involved in a public controversy in front of the boss and others? Might not people assigned the con side win people over and undermine motivation to develop teamwork at Community Bank?

Leslie agreed to work with Daniel to see if they could develop a practical approach to using advocacy teams to introduce and practice open-mindedness. She argued that advocacy groups give the okay to disagree and provide a format to help make it constructive. She has seen students and employees use advocacy teams to have intense, informed discussions.

> Two weeks later and after the training session that Daniel and Leslie had led on advocacy teams, Joel wanted to talk about it with his colleagues. He began by teasing Thomas, "I saw you really getting into the controversy yesterday. You were on the attack, I almost felt sorry for your partner."
>
> "I enjoyed it," Thomas conceded. "Actually we both had points we wanted to make."
>
> "I was wondering what happened to our peaceful Asian," Joel said.
>
> "You should stop by our home when you are in New York, you could see the whole family arguing," Thomas said. "We're even louder than the workshop."

"I enjoyed the controversy too," Courtney said. "We weren't loud in our group but we had points to refute as well as make. You liked the controversy too, right?"

"Interesting," Joel said. "But as with the murder mystery, the situation was kind of artificial. We were supposed to disagree. We were told to disagree."

"That's part of the exercise," Thomas said. "Disagreeing can be very useful, we need to practice disagreeing respectfully."

"Leslie said that controversy can help us be more open ourselves," Courtney said. "Telling our ideas can help us listen to others' ideas. That's interesting."

"Yes, when we don't speak our minds, we can be less open to listening to others," Thomas said.

"Listening is the hardest part," Joel said. "Not so difficult to develop arguments even for the pro side, but difficult to re-state my partner's con arguments. I forgot to listen."

"Listening is harder than talking," Thomas said.

"We have to practice that part more," Courtney said. "It's easy to think you are listening, only to find out that you cannot restate the other's arguments."

"It looks like we'll have a lot of practice," Thomas said. "We're supposed to be open-minded so that we can manage ourselves."

"Our so-called leaders are pushing more things off their desks and onto our laps," Joel said.

"But we want to manage ourselves, right?" Courtney said. "You complain about Gregory micro-managing and jumping into making decisions he knows little about."

"I've been known to make this point," Joel said. "We already self-manage. We make decisions without telling Gregory. Getting his suggestions just wastes time."

"Sometimes when he does tell us his ideas, we ignore him," Thomas said.

"We have to do what we think is right," Joel said. "Who wants to follow a dumb decision that we don't understand. No one wants to be stupid."

"We'll face more pressure to make good decisions," Courtney said. "We better know more about how to discuss open-mindedly."

"Leslie is sending us more materials on how we can develop our team's open-mindedness," Joel said.

"Study together, do together," Thomas said.

Working Together

Joel, his teammates, and other colleagues at Community Bank were realizing that while teamwork could both strengthen them as individuals and get important things done for the bank, they had to be persistent and skilled to develop teamwork. In addition to cooperative relationships, they had to work together daily. To sell more profitable loans, Joel, Thomas, and Courtney should combine their ideas and develop new, attractive offers that respond to customers' needs as well as meet the standards of the risk managers at the bank. These were challenging tasks that required their integrated consideration and effort.

Teams are composed of distinct individuals with their own preferences, aspirations, and habits so that team members must develop their ways of relating and working with each other so as to fit them. Team members change their moods and motivation so that working with a team member this week is not exactly like the previous week. Team membership changes; working with one marketing specialist is not like working with another. These demands seem to be growing as organizations develop new structures and procedures to respond to rapid changes in markets and turnover.

Joel and his teammates were realizing that they needed to manage their internal workings so that they continue to combine their ideas and efforts as well as monitor their environment. Even with a genuine consensus on targets and a clear division of labor and roles, there is no plan of action that ensures effective coordination and team success. Things change, issues come up, and new opportunities arise. Coordinating team members requires ongoing adaptation and decision making.

Cooperative goals help team members discuss their various views open-mindedly for mutual benefit. Through this open-minded discussion, team members identify issues, develop solutions, and implement decisions to strengthen their coordination and complete their tasks.

Leader Roles: From Making Decisions to Promoting Team Decision Making

Leaders have traditionally considered their role to be one of making decisions, especially tough ones. Their responsibility and contribution to their team and organization is to decide and implement. Leaders have an overall view and organizational perspective, the relevant information and knowledge, and the power and authority to command compliance. Leaders think and decide, employees act and implement.

This traditional view of leaders as decision makers is becoming less credible. Decision making is much more than making a decision! Problems must be recognized and analyzed; alternatives must be created and prioritized; realistic plans for implementing solutions developed; and solutions must be flexibly carried out. But knowledge and information are distributed over many people, not held solely by the manager. Employees themselves have relevant knowledge and are often in a good position to apply it effectively. Managers have general knowledge and perspective that are useful but insufficient for today's important, complex problems.

Leaders should work with and through others as they make decisions. Leaders are effective decision makers when they develop high quality relationships and open-minded discussions with and among employees.

ADVOCACY TEAMS

Open-minded discussions should become part of the culture of Community Bank and other organizations. Managers can use advocacy teams to show staff how they can use opposing ideas for mutual benefit. Advocacy teams can resolve major issues where employees have developed strong preferences. They can also begin a discussion on issues that employees have not yet but should consider. Advocacy teams can be structured to take 15 minutes, two hours, even weeks depending on the subject and objectives. For example, staff might be given a week to develop and defend their position regarding whether to purchase another company; the controversy itself may take several meetings. Structuring advocacy teams is a practical, flexible way to develop open-minded discussions.

Steps include:

1. Inform colleagues that they are asked to disagree with each other so that they can learn more about controversy and make the best decision possible.
2. Form employees into groups of four.
3. Propose distinct conclusions and courses of action for the problem under consideration. Assign two group members to be an advocacy team to present the best case possible for the pro position and the other two for the con position.
4. Each advocacy pair researches its position and prepares a persuasive presentation of their position to convince others it is valid. Working in pairs, they help each other develop a plan about how to present their case and in other ways get ready to defend their assigned position. Each person should have a copy of the plan, as each person will defend the assigned position.
5. Switch partners so that there is a pro and con person in the new pairs.
6. The pro person presents the pro's case forcefully. The con person presents the con's case forcefully. They disagree openly

with each other, finding weaknesses in the other's position, defending their own and developing new arguments.

7. They demonstrate that they understand the opposing position by re-stating the other's arguments accurately and sincerely.

8. Pairs stop defending their assigned positions. They take the best ideas from both positions to create alternatives and then decide on the solution that they both believe is most effective.

9. The group of four re-forms and compares the integrated solutions developed in each pair.

10. Groups of four compare their solutions and, if appropriate, decide on the best solutions.

11. Staff re-form their group of four to reflect on the controversy. They identify ways that they liked about how they disagreed with each other and develop at least one way that they could improve.

12. They thank their group members for helping them prepare to disagree, for disagreeing with them, and combining their ideas.

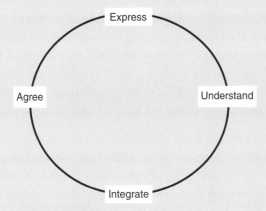

FIG 7.1 / **Open-minded discussion**

The Potential of Teams

Even when recognizing the limits of one-person rule, many people have been suspicious of teams, doubting that they are much of an answer for how to decide difficult issues in organizations. However, research has convincingly documented two important conclusions. First, teams have considerable potential to solve problems and make decisions. Second, teams must be well structured and managed to realize their potential. High quality relationships and discussion among team members and leaders are needed to take advantage of the potential of team decision making.

Patrick Laughlin (2011) of the University of Illinois conducted research that develops our understanding of the potential of team decision making. In a series of careful experiments, he compared different memberships, tasks, and abilities of members to document how groups make decisions. These findings all converge to a single, powerful conclusion: In teams, "truth wins." If one person in a group has an excellent insight, all team members are apt to develop the insight.

The stereotype is that groups sink to the lowest common denominator; they pool ignorance and average member's responses. However, Laughlin's studies show that team members can and do discriminate; they do not simply average their ideas but identify the best ideas and information and combine this knowledge into their decisions. Less insightful team members, though they do not produce a good answer to a problem, typically recognize a good answer. They willingly relinquish their inferior ideas, especially if they can be shown the logic of the superior answer.

Evidence, though, does not show that groups are always superior to individuals making decisions alone. Individuals can solve some problems quite efficiently. For example, individuals were found to be more effective at responding to computer simulated air attacks than groups (Beersman, Hollenbeck, Humphrey, Moon, and Ilgen, 2003). Individuals had sufficient information and could respond quickly and accurately. Consulting with a team member did not provide much useful new information and slowed decision-making time.

These results remind us that leaders should not assign all tasks and problems to a team. As discussed in Chapters 4 and 6, teams should have challenging tasks that require teammates to pool their information and integrate their ideas. Some tasks do not call for such effort. Indeed, well-functioning teams assign straightforward tasks to individuals. One team member agrees to be responsible for arranging the room, another for the refreshments, and a third for publicity; together they will develop the agenda and program for the conference.

Teams for Crises Too

Many people argue that leaders cannot rely on teams in a crisis; they have to make quick, decisive decisions, not let teams dither and contemplate. The speed of business today increasingly requires fast decisions by bright individuals at the top. Studies, however, show that managers and employees rely on teamwork even more in crises. Crisis may call for quick decisions, but also for thoughtful ones; followers want to be sure the decisions will help them through the crisis.

We placed managers in three experimental conditions and asked them to make a high quality decision (Tjosvold, 1984). Mangers who believed that the situation was a crisis made little effort to listen or understand their employees, and consequently made inferior decisions. Managers who considered the problem as minor and insignificant acted similarly in that they also made little effort to understand their employees' ideas and feelings and made inferior decisions. However, managers who saw the situation as a challenge that required a thoughtful response open-mindedly consulted with their employees and made high quality decisions.

To examine crisis decision making in field settings, pilots, first officers, and flight attendants were interviewed as they dealt with such threats as an engine falling off (Tjosvold, 1990). Unlike the stereotype that the pilot takes over, we found that flight crew members consulted quickly with each other, discussed options, and worked together to reach an agreement. To the extent that they had cooperative goals, they were more open to express their own and to listen to each other's ideas and suggestions and the more effectively they restored the margin of safety to the airplane.

Dramatic cases studies also support the reliance on team decision making in the cockpit. For example, a flight attendant on an Air Ontario flight did not confront the pilot with her observation that there was ice on the wings, which she knew might interfere with the plane's ability to gain altitude. The plane crashed 15 seconds after takeoff and 24 people died. The diagnosis "pilot error" as a cause of airplane crashes often means that pilots, first officers, and flight attendants did not share their information and ideas efficiently.

Moving to Team Decision Making

Successful leaders do not try to be "right" by identifying problems and creating the best solution themselves. Even when making decisions themselves, wise managers consult with others. In our study of managers in Shanghai, those who felt uncertain about their individual decision consulted with their colleagues (Tjosvold, Peng, Chen, and Su 2012). When they consulted open-mindedly, managers clarified their own thinking and made high quality decisions. Individuals contribute to team decision making, but the team can contribute to individual decision making.

Savvy managers fulfill their decision-making role by helping the team to be "right" in creating and implementing high quality solutions to the key issues and problems the team and organization face. They help employees discuss open-mindedly so that they identify issues that need attention, dig into them to identify frustrating barriers and potential advantages, create potential solutions, and then choose and implement solutions.

Whether teams should manage themselves without the involvement of managers has been discussed for decades. Some organizations are experimenting with self-managing teams where there is no formal leader and the team "leads" itself by refining its goals and methods. The team is expected to decide; there is no leader to rely upon.

The reality is that all teams must, to some extent, manage their internal affairs. Managers are seldom able to know all relevant team developments or in a position to make ongoing decisions. Similarly, team members typically need to know about the developments in the organization and marketplace that their managers often have knowledge of.

Team members should then also consult open-mindedly with managers as well as discuss open-mindedly with each other as they make decisions and manage themselves. Evidence confirms that team members who discuss issues open-mindedly are able to make effective use of the opportunity of self-managing to maintain their relationships and get things done (Alper, Tjosvold, and Law, 1998, 2000).

Team decision making must be skillfully conducted to take advantage of its potential. Leaders should develop cooperative relationships that involve employees effectively in making decisions, specifically so that they discuss their diverse views open-mindedly. They recognize that what is important is that the team makes the right decision, not them, and that their role is to help the team succeed. The next section shows how open-minded discussion is useful for decision making.

Open-minded Discussion for Team Decision Making

Diverse members and ideas are a fundamental part of working with others. As discussed in Chapter 4, diversity can be highly useful if managed effectively. Different ideas and opinions discussed open-mindedly help teams find quality solutions they want to implement.

The open-minded discussion of diverse views for mutual benefit is a powerful way to characterize how team members can work together continually. Teammates who open-mindedly exchange their views can refine their ways of working together. They identify frustrations and implement new ways. They can manage themselves so that they continue to work together to get things done.

We are not arguing that open-minded consideration should be given to every issue and every decision. Some decisions are too minor and do not justify people's time and effort. However, open-mindedness should be the underlying way of working with each other, especially with issues that are important to the team's progress and to individual team members.

Open-minded discussion comes in many shapes and forms. Sometimes team members can discuss issues very quickly seemingly without much debate. Teams and their leaders should identify issues that are vital enough to require considerable open-minded discussion whereas minor issues can be dealt with quickly.

As they begin to disagree over a problem, decision makers state and explain their own position and ideas. They rebut counter-arguments and elaborate, but they also come to doubt the wisdom and correctness of their own position. Listening to opposing ideas creates internal, cognitive conflict questioning whether one original position is as useful and sensible as first assumed. With this uncertainty they actively search for new information. They question their protagonists to clarify their positions and rephrase their arguments so that they can understand the opposing position more thoroughly. The elaboration and search leaves people open-minded and knowledgeable about the issue. They have approached the issue from several perspectives and are not rigidly fixed to their own.

With open-mindedness, decision makers synthesize different ideas and facts into new positions not previously considered. The increase in the number and quality of ideas and higher levels of stimulation facilitates creativity. This open-mindedness fosters a camaraderie that reinforces commitment to the group's position. People have fully voiced their opinions, listened to each other, and enjoyed the excitement of disagreeing together. They feel better about themselves and about their team members.

Team members and their leaders can be encouraged to develop the skills and procedures of open-minded discussion. It has four mutually reinforcing aspects: Develop and express own ideas, question and understand other views, integrate and create new ideas, and agree and implement a solution (Johnson, Johnson, and Tjosvold, 2006; Tjosvold, 1985). These dynamics suggest the challenges of discussing issues open-mindedly and how managers and employees can develop their skills to discuss conflict constructively.

PITFALLS OF LEADERS' CLOSE SUPERVISION

Leaders often make decisions for the team about how members should coordinate and work together as well as how to get tasks done. They have useful perspectives; they can be particularly insightful in helping the team understand what the organization and customers expect of them. But leaders themselves are often not in a very good position to understand and resolve many relationship and task issues faced by teams.

Close supervision, decried as micro-managing, often frustrates employees. Telling team members what to do does not mean that they understand or are motivated to do it. Effective coordination among team members requires ongoing decision making and adjusting; it's too complex for the leader to decide alone. Close supervision is especially ineffective for taking advantage of new opportunities and responding to changes.

Team management where members are actively involved in solving problems and making decisions is a solid basis for effective teamwork. Team members have the information, insight, and motivation to discuss and decide many issues. Better to have all team members be vigilant and involved in keeping the team on course than just the leader.

Develop and Express Own Views

Expressing one's own needs, feelings, and ideas very much contributes to open-minded discussion. Team members need to know what each other wants and believes is valuable in order to develop resolutions that they all believe are mutually beneficial and constructive. A climate that helps team members feel safe to speak their minds very much contributes to teamwork (Edmondson, 2012).

To strengthen expression of their own position, team members can learn to research their position, present the best case they can for it, and defend it vigorously. They learn to be effective advocates, persuasively presenting the best case possible for their positions. They also practice to be effective devil's advocates, critically analyzing opposing positions, pointing out their weaknesses and flaws with evidence and logic. They learn to refute opposing views vigorously to highlight the strength of their own position. However, expressing one's own position needs to be supplemented with openness to the other's position.

Question and Understand Other Views

Disagreeing is an opportunity to know opposing positions as well as to develop and express one's own. Listening and understanding opposing views as well as defending one's own makes discussing issues more challenging but also more rewarding.

Team members learn to refute the opposing positions but in ways that foster more discussion. They point out weaknesses in each other's arguments to encourage everyone to develop and express their positions by finding more evidence and strengthening their reasoning. They identify weaknesses in the other's position while communicating that they want the other to strengthen the defense of his or her position.

Team members become less certain that their original position is adequate and complete and seek to understand opposing views. They learn to ask questions for more information about the logic and evidence supporting opposing views. They act on their curiosity by stopping the denfense of their own position in order to ask questions about other views (Tjosvold and Johnson 1977, 1978).

Role reversal asks team members to put themselves in each other's shoes and to present the opposing arguments as comprehensively and convincing as they can (Johnson 1967, 1971a, b). These re-statements of the opposing views communicate that the protagonists are listening to each other as well as deepening their understanding of the opposing position.

Integrate and Create Solutions

The creation of new alternatives lays the foundations for genuine agreement to a solution that team members accept and implement. Open-minded discussion helps them develop and evaluate alternative resolutions so that they can implement the one they believe is most effective. They also may develop more confidence in their relationships as they have exchanged views directly and show that they are trying to understand and integrate each other's ideas so that all benefit.

Team members may, however, have to engage in repeated discussions to reach an agreement or, indeed, they may be unable to create a solution that is mutually acceptable. They may, for example, be unconvinced that the evidence warrants modifying their original positions. They may have to continue to discuss their opposing views until they develop a mutually beneficial resolution.

Agree and Implement Solutions

Open-minded discussion has been found to contribute to the full, effective participation and mutual influence (Tjosvold 1987; Tjosvold and Field 1983). Laboratory and field experiments have shown that individuals involved in controversial participation reach agreement and carry out that agreement (Richter & Tjosvold 1980; Tjosvold and Deemer 1980).

Teams and organizations can develop supportive norms and patterns to help team members be open with their ideas, open to other views, and integrate them. Managers and employees understand that they should seek the best reasoned judgment, not winning; they criticize ideas, not people; they listen and learn everyone's position, even if they do not agree with it; they differentiate positions before trying to integrate them; and they change their mind when logically persuaded to do so.

Closing Comments

Developing strong cooperative goals, forming diverse teams, sitting knee-to-knee and eye-to-eye, and getting to know each other are foundations for productive teamwork, but team members must actually coordinate and work together. Teams have the potential to contribute to organizations and people because they can combine the diverse capabilities and work of members. To realize this potential, team members must develop goals and plans, identify opportunities and pitfalls, and resolve issues. Teams must continually make high quality decisions about how to coordinate their work and about the best way to reach their work goals.

Open-minded discussions are key for how team members can manage themselves (Tjosvold, Wong, and Chen, 2014; Alper et al., 1998; 2000). Without open-mindedness, team members fail to integrate their diverse ideas and abilities effectively, undermining their teamwork as well as their productivity. This chapter utilized research to provide a crisp understanding of the nature of open-minded discussion, giving team members a common ideal for how they should work together. Teams then resolve task and relationship issues creatively and efficiently to be productive in the long term.

Action Plans

Do less of:

- Find a solution quickly, skip understanding the problem.
- Reject ideas because they come from unexpected sources.
- Dismiss ideas that cannot be quickly justified.
- Pretend to listen.
- Use other's arguments only to strengthen your position.
- Convey you are right, others wrong.

Do more of:

- Understand the problem, and then develop solutions.
- Discuss the value of an open-minded discussion of views.
- Use advocacy teams to structure open-minded discussions.
- Develop and express everyone's views.
- Question to understand other views.
- Put yourself in other's shoes.
- Integrate views to create solutions.
- Agree and implement solutions.
- Reflect on how the team discussed their ideas and develop plans to improve.
- Celebrate success in discussing views open-mindedly.

8

chapter

Managing Conflict Constructively

When a minister lives among calumniators, flatterers, and sycophants, though he may wish the state to be well governed, is it possible for it to be so?

Confucius

Thomas came out of his office when he saw Courtney in the common area. "I've been frustrated the whole morning," he said. "I've been trying to get some things done but I keep thinking about how angry I am with Joel. I've been working on the Donaldson loan for weeks, meeting them, playing golf, and knowing them and their business. I was getting a better understanding of what they want from a bank and from their loan. That is what we are supposed to be doing, right? Understand our customers."

Courtney had seen Thomas angry before but not very often and not very much. She said, "What happened? You and Joel were to meet with them this morning, to more or less close the deal, I thought."

"That's what I thought," Thomas responded. "Joel was to assure them that I wasn't alone and was representing the bank, that Joel and by implication the bank as a whole, were keen to do business with them and could provide the kind of loan that fits them. I had briefed Joel, told him what I learned, and why my proposed loan structure works for them and for the bank."

"I was there when you told him at our weekly meeting," Courtney said.

"Glad you remember, Joel was only there in body. I still can't believe it; he talked to the Donaldson group like we're just beginning to discuss the loan and brainstorm possibilities. He went on and on about why they should seriously consider a loan with low initiation fees and upfront costs but with a slightly higher interest rate.

"I had told Joel that we have already had that discussion. They don't like paying high interests rates. They have the cash on hand now and would rather pay up front and then carry a low interest loan. It fits the values and habits of the founders. But it is reasonable too. This kind of loan helps them with their income management.

"We're supposed to be a team and help each other. He knows that I have taken the lead working with Donaldson and he's to support me. If he doesn't like my way of proceeding with them, he should say that at our team meeting and in the office, not wait to surprise me at a client meeting, when the only thing I can do is keep quiet and look down. I can't fight him in front of the customers. He was more than annoying, more than an aggravation."

Courtney was not quite sure what to say but wanted to say something helpful. "I knew it must be important for you to be so upset. You don't get angry easily."

"I don't want to be angry," Thomas said. "But there are times when being angry is called for. What was he trying to do? Trying to be the all-knowing boss?"

"I wonder too," Courtney said. "He could have thought that as a Senior VP he had to contribute, say something. Perhaps he wanted to show Donaldson that he too was customer oriented. Not sure what was on his mind; we have to ask him."

"Ask him?" Thomas said. "Don't think so. How would I do that?"

"You can talk to him about this, let him know what you're thinking," Courtney said. "You, we, don't want this to happen again, right?"

"I don't," Thomas said. "I think he should ask me."

"He could but he might not," Courtney said.

"We're supposed to be a team, we're supposed to cooperate together," Thomas said.

"That's why you should talk to him," Courtney said. "You didn't work together well but you want to do so in the future so you want to iron out difficulties. Talking to him soon seems better than later."

"Sounds idealistic," Thomas said. "I doubt that I can do that with him, especially now that I'm angry."

"I'm not suggesting that you yell and scream at him," Courtney said. "But he should know you're angry. You can't expect him to guess correctly, especially about why you're angry and what he did that got you angry."

"But he should know, he's suppose to be our team leader," Thomas said.

"Maybe he should, but maybe he doesn't," Courtney said. "He might well feel that he was helpful and you should thank him for his help."

"I won't do that," Thomas said

"He might expect you to say thank you," Courtney said. "Crazier things have happened."

"How should I tell him?" Thomas asked.

"Remember, we're to discuss issues open-mindedly," Courtney said. "Tell him you want to talk with him about the Donaldson visit and ask him when you can talk. Let's plan what to do."

Thomas developed some confidence that Courtney and he had worked out a practical plan. He texted Joel, asking him if they could discuss the Donaldson meeting. He indicated that he had concerns about the meeting so that Joel would not be caught off guard. Joel agreed to meet that afternoon.

After greetings and sitting knee-to-knee, eye-to-eye, Thomas told Joel that he wanted to express his ideas and feelings directly to him and hoped they could discuss what happened together open-mindedly. He was irritated with Joel because he thought they had worked out a plan for how to build upon his work and relationship with Donaldson. But Joel took the initiative and did his own thing by pushing alternative loan proposals.

"Thought I was helping," Joel said. "I was trying to show that we're oriented toward the customers and want them to have choices."

"You neglected all my prior work with them, it was like I hadn't been meeting with them and talking about options and moving forward to closing the deal," Thomas said.

"I didn't mean any harm," Joel said. "I was just trying to be a helpful team member and a good client oriented sales person."

"You didn't listen to me at the team meeting when I reported the real progress I had made," Thomas said. "It's as if you don't care what I've done."

Joel was unsure how to respond to these accusations. He did not want to admit a mistake as he thought his actions weren't that bad and certainly were well intended. "I just don't think that the Donaldson people were upset, they all seemed interested and quite friendly when I left."

"They're friendly people, they are always friendly, but I could tell that they were ambiguous and less sure of what kind of loan they wanted," Thomas said. "They thought less of me, wondered whether I really spoke for the bank."

"Oh, I think you're exaggerating, it's not so bad, no reason to feel sorry for yourself," Joel said trying to console Thomas.

Thomas was not consoled. "I am not exaggerating. I'm angry. You made me look bad in front of clients, you frustrated closing the deal with them, and now you're telling me I'm exaggerating."

Joel was now even less confident about how to respond. "Are you sure the Donaldson's people feel that way?" But he knew right after he spoke that he was adding fuel to the conflict, not cooling it down.

"Am I supposed to ask them at the meeting whether you made me look like a weak person and an ineffectual banker?" Thomas said. "You need absolute proof, do you? Should they sign a document testifying to their feelings?"

Joel was trying to think of a way out of this discussion, or at least to make it less hot. Then he remembered that trying to understand the other's view was an important, though often neglected, part of openness. He thought that showing he was trying to understand Thomas would be a good teamwork option for him. Perhaps he could even make this situation more constructive. "Okay, I'll stop defending myself and try to understand you."

"Good idea," Thomas said in a slightly less irritated tone.

But Joel could not resist defending himself more. "Really, believe me that I was trying to be helpful, I wasn't trying to make you look ineffective in front of Donaldson. I was not trying to show you any disrespect. That would be stupid, we're a team."

Thomas was still irritated but he also welcomed this assurance. He wanted to avoid letting his anger get out of control and blame Joel too harshly. Everyone makes mistakes and after all the goal of the discussion was to work more effectively with Joel in the future. He said, "I hope you didn't mean to."

"You're irritated with me because you think that I wasn't recognizing your contributions, and not listening to you before we meet with Donaldson, as if I didn't respect you," Joel said trying to practice demonstrating his understanding of Thomas.

Thomas was still irritated and he repeated his grievances against Joel but with less force. Joel reminded himself that he had already told Thomas that he did not intend to show any disrespect. There was no reason for him to keep repeating it. He saw that showing that he was now listening to Thomas was a viable option.

After five more minutes of venting and discussing, Thomas was less angry and Joel less stressed. "I don't have too much more to say," Thomas said. "I think you have heard me out and the reasons why I got angry. Hopefully, this kind of thing won't happen again in the future."

"I hope so too," Joel said. "You have made your points directly and forcefully, I can remember. I should listen better before client meetings and I can be more aware of what team members have already contributed. But I might need reminders."

"I suppose we can all use reminders, but reminding is not an easy job, at least for me," Thomas said.

"I appreciate you letting me know your feelings and ideas, now I can be a more alert teammate," Joel said.

"I appreciate your willingness to meet and your openness," Thomas said.

Joel then realized he could apologize genuinely. "I'm really sorry that I didn't show you enough respect at the meeting."

"I accept your apology," Thomas said. "Thank you. And thanks for listening to my anger."

"Perhaps you can tell my family that I can apologize," Joel tried to end with some humor and to move away from being the target of anger. "How about I take you and Courtney to lunch later this week?"

"Good idea," Thomas said as he left the office.

Feeling in Conflict

Thomas was angry that Joel did not recognize and respect his work on the Donaldson loan. Joel too was upset because he thought Thomas did not appreciate that he was working to be a good team member and supporting Thomas. Both Thomas and Joel wanted to be team members who help each other succeed, but they frustrated each other.

Wanting to help each team member succeed is an important foundation for productive teamwork but it is insufficient. With common tasks and shared rewards, teammates may conclude that they have cooperative goals and discuss issues open-mindedly to develop practical plans to coordinate their work to complete their tasks. However, they still have conflict. Team members disagree as they develop plans and as they implement them and coordinate their work. They may feel frustrated by how they treat each other as individuals. But as Joel, Thomas, and Courtney were learning, teammates can discuss their conflicts to strengthen their teamwork.

Understanding Conflict

Thomas and Joel were both reluctant to discuss their conflict with each other. An underlying reason was their lingering notion that good teammates should not have conflict. Conflicts are signs that teammates have let

each other down and made mistakes; discussing these cases only aggra-
vates bad feelings. Thomas was hoping to find a way to steady himself
and reduce his frustration so that he could get work done and move away
from feeling mistreated. Joel was upset too because he thought Thomas
was unfairly accusing him of being an irresponsible team member; Thomas
should appreciate his efforts, not scold him.

Fortunately, they had been studying teamwork. They were realizing that
conflict and teamwork go together and that working cooperatively does
not mean avoiding conflicts, but discussing them open-mindedly to aid their
joint work. Courtney was in a position to remind Thomas of these ideas as
well as to provide concrete help to develop a plan to manage conflict.

Many managers and employees share Thomas' and Joel's confusion that
conflict and cooperation are opposites. Conflict researchers have traditionally defined conflict as opposing interests involving scarce resources and
goal divergence and frustration. Defining conflict as opposing interests
reinforces the popular assumption that conflicts are not just about differences but are win–lose struggles that require harsh, aggressive action. To
many, conflict is the opposite of cooperation and teamwork; conflict is
"one against another", even a war. Assuming that conflict is competitive
and the opposite of cooperation makes managing conflict constructively
very difficult.

Defining conflict as opposing interests obscures that people with com-
pletely compatible goals not only can, but also often, have conflict. It con-
founds conflict with competition defined as incompatible goals. Thomas
and Joel were in conflict although both of them wanted to develop a
strong customer relationship with Donaldson. They had cooperative goals
but they had incompatible actions. Joel was proposing alternative options
for Donaldson whereas Thomas was working to gain final acceptance of a
loan agreement. They were both committed to developing a high quality
approach to their customer but had different ideas about the nature of a
high quality approach.

Deutsch (1973) clarified that conflict involves incompatible activities;
one person's actions interfere, obstruct, or somehow get in the way

of another's action. Incompatible activities occur in both cooperation and competition. Whether protagonists believe their goals are cooperative or competitive very much affects their expectations, interaction, and outcomes in conflict.

Traditional ideas that conflict develops from opposing interests reinforce rather than challenge popular misconceptions and attitudes about conflict. Team members should reject that conflicts necessarily involve competitive, negatively related goals. Defining conflict as incompatible activities can help develop more realistic and useful understanding and feelings toward conflict.

Conflict is Everywhere and Everywhere Can Be Valuable

Thomas and Joel were not only uncertain about how conflict fits in with cooperative teamwork, they were not confident in what discussing conflict would contribute. Courtney appreciated more clearly that their discussing the conflict directly would be much more useful than avoiding it.

Researchers emphasize two fundamental conclusions about conflict management. First, conflict pervades social and organizational life; to work in an organization is to be in conflict. Managers, for example, have been estimated to spend 30–40 per cent of their typical workday addressing workplace conflicts and as much as 80 per cent of the difficulties they face are based on strained relationships with employees (Dana, 2005).

Second, researchers have concluded that discussing and managing conflict can very much promote productivity, strengthen relationships, and enhance people. Well-managed conflict accomplishes tasks and prepares collaborators to be successful in the future. There is no realistic alternative to managing conflict.

Conflict management has traditionally been considered an aberration from hierarchical, well functioning organizational behavior, but studies show that conflict extends throughout organizational work and promotes vital organizational outcomes. Avoiding conflict, though useful in some circumstances, is ineffectual as a general approach toward collaborating (Tjosvold, 1991, 2007). Wishing for a "conflict-free" work environment is unrealistic and pretending to be conflict free is undesirable.

Working with others and managing conflict are inseparable; dealing with conflict is not an activity separate from work. Managing conflict is part of leadership, teamwork, and decision making. Leaders and team members have been shown to be continually confronted with conflict and must manage that conflict to work successfully in accounting, marketing, human resources, indeed, all areas of organizations.

Conflict Management for Productivity

Conflict management gets many diverse things done (Tjosvold, Wong, and Chen, 2014). Managed conflict promotes team performance and citizenship behavior. When employees discussed their views openly and constructively, they reduced costs and improved quality, used new technology advantageously and made restructuring effective. Top management teams who managed their conflicts cooperatively developed their company's innovation and strategic advantages. Conflict management helps entrepreneurs strengthen their networks so that they can develop their business.

Conflict Management for Learning

Conflict management promotes learning as team members begin to doubt the adequacy of their present ideas and search to understand and develop perspectives that may be more adequate (Johnson, Johnson, and Tjosvold, 2014). Students who disagreed with each other checked out more books from the library and demonstrated greater understanding of the issues than students without conflict. By managing conflict cooperatively, teams are able to reflect on their experiences to improve performance.

Developmental psychologists have long argued that controversy induces taking each other's perspective that in turn promotes moral and cognitive development. Evidence documents the value of cooperative conflict for psychological wellbeing. Employees in China predisposed to manage conflict open-mindedly and integratively were psychologically healthy both in terms of general and work-specific measures (Tjosvold, Huang, Johnson, and Johnson, 2008). Being predisposed to resolve conflicts in win–lose ways seemed to have at least some benefits for long-term psychological health. But avoiding conflict was not useful for either general or work-related health outcomes and resulted in alienation from work and co-workers.

Managing Conflicts over Interests and Emotions

The value of discussing conflict open-mindedly is not limited to decisions and differences of opinions but is also useful for conflicts involving interests. For example, management and union representatives with cooperative goals expressed their opposing views directly to each other, listened open-mindedly, conveyed an intention to work for mutual benefit, and combined their ideas (Tjosvold, Morishima, and Belsheim, 1999; Tjosvold, and Morishima, 1999). With this kind of discussion, they developed creative, quality solutions and used their resources efficiently. They resolved their grievances with positive feelings, satisfied both union and management, and improved procedures that would help them resolve future grievances.

Despite the widespread beliefs that conflict's benefits are limited to task and rational issues, studies indicate that managing emotions and interpersonal tensions can be constructive. For example, open-minded discussions of anger strengthened relationships and restored respect between teammates (Tjosvold, 2002; Tjosvold, and Su, 2007). Through these discussions, the angered persons communicated that they believed their teammate had intentionally and without justification, frustrated them and explained their reasons for feeling angry. Teammates then clarified their intentions, apologized, and made amends and thereby developed confidence that similar incidents are less likely to occur again.

Managing conflict is more than an opportunity to get an agreement; it is also a means for teams to coordinate diverse actions and integrate contrasting ideas into creative solutions. Conflict, when skillfully managed, promotes productivity, people, and relationships.

Teambuilding for Conflict Management

Working to apply the model of cooperative goals and open-minded discussion did not prevent conflict within their team, but it helped Joel, Thomas, and Courtney learn to manage their conflict. As they felt that they were in this together, they had some confidence that they were all prepared to try to use the conflict for mutual benefit. They understood that strengthening their relationships was valuable and useful for themselves and their work. They could see that simply avoiding conflict and pretending to agree with each other were ineffective and that they should use conflict to strengthen their cooperative relationships.

Their team building experience helped them have a specific understanding of how they could manage conflict. They were learning to make conflict constructive by discussing it open-mindedly. They should express their views and their reasons behind their views directly and fully. They should also use the conflict to understand the other's position. Then they can integrate their best ideas into a workable solution.

Many people think that they, but not others, are prepared to manage conflict. But as they were studying the teamwork model together, Joel, Thomas, and Courtney had a common understanding and commitment upon which they could make good use of their conflict. Courtney had the confidence to provide suggestions knowing that Thomas and Joel would appreciate her logic. All three had these experiences so that they believed their partners were oriented toward strengthening their cooperative relationships and discussing their opposing views open-mindedly.

LEADERS FROM CONFLICT ARBITRATORS TO CONFLICT MEDIATORS

As he was developing a team organization, Daniel was moving Community Bank from relying on leader-dominated conflict management to team conflict management. Rather than act as an arbitrator, Daniel wanted to be a mediator who helps employees handle their own conflicts.

Arbitration is a viable approach to managing conflicts. Supply partners worldwide have asked courts of arbitration to resolve contract and other business disputes more quickly and cheaply than traditional legal means. Organizations, unions, and employees as well as companies and customers have also used formal arbitration to settle their disputes.

Arbitrators take an unbiased role to become familiar with the problem and opposing positions and to examine all the evidence with the objective to render a judgment about how the conflict should be resolved. After conflict, partners agree that they will abide by the arbitrator's decision, they submit their positions and how they want the conflict to be resolved. Each side has a full opportunity to present its case and then refute and provide counter evidence to the other side's arguments. They try to persuade the arbitrator through facts and logic; then the arbitrator announces the decision and its rationale.

In addition to this formal arbitration, informal arbitration is very common within organizations; indeed, it is typically the method of choice in dealing with a wide range of conflicts. In a traditional hierarchy, managers have the authority and responsibility to settle disputes and ensure smooth coordination. Passing a conflict up the hierarchy to be resolved is, after avoiding, perhaps the most popular way to deal with conflict in organizations.

Arbitration fits the traditional view of the leader as solving problems and making decisions. It can seem more efficient than having teammates discuss their conflicts. However, informal arbitration in organizations is often implemented in abbreviated, ineffective ways.

Managers can easily bring strong attitudes and biases toward the conflict partners and their conflict. Feeling they do not have the time to proceed through the steps of arbitration thoroughly, managers are tempted to short-circuit the process, for example, by making a decision after listening to one side. They dismiss preparing positions as time wasting brooding and refuting each other's arguments as squabbling. Employees are upset but are embarrassed to discuss their position with their manager. The result is that informal arbitration often results in low quality solutions with employee feelings left unresolved.

Arbitration is overused and mediation is underused in organizations. Although both can be useful and dysfunctional, mediation when employing cooperative conflict management provides more face-to-face opportunities to present and understand each other's point of view, create new alternatives, and reach an agreement that team members believe is fair and effective. Rather than try to arbitrate conflicts one by one, managers can have a powerful impact on conflict management through developing cooperative relationships and open-minded discussions that employees can use to manage their own conflicts.

Challenges to Manage Conflict

Although studies in the West and the East have documented that many people in a wide range of settings are able to use conflict effectively, conflicts are often poorly managed. Managing conflict challenges people and their relationships. Life involves give and take; conflict presses us to do these fully and skillfully.

To discuss their views open-mindedly, teammates must be both emotional and rational; they should express their feelings but also develop their arguments rationally using deductive and inductive reasoning. They must honestly express their own views but do so in ways that encourage others to express theirs. Putting oneself in another's shoes is difficult to do, especially in the heat of an intense conflict. Incorporating opposing arguments into one's own thinking requires moving away from one's original position and re-thinking one's arguments. Unfortunately, we are typically more skilled at resolving minor conflicts than more vital ones.

Conflict management is a joint activity, much more effective when all sides believe they are trying to make their conflicts mutually beneficial. But these expectations are fragile as people misread each other's intentions. Avoiding a discussion can be intended to minimize the other's discomfort but be experienced as closed-mindedness. Arguing a position forcefully can be intended to initiate an open dialogue but be experienced as an attempt to coerce.

Many traditional organizational values and practices frustrate constructive conflict management. Leaders have been thought to exert their decisive role by minimizing conflict and eliminating it quickly to develop a harmonious, efficient department; they were to step in to any conflict and find a quick solution that restored the department's efficiency. Employees are expected to be rational and not let feelings interfere, but conflict stimulates emotions that require expression and management.

Cooperative relationships are an important condition for productive conflict management but many relationships in organizations are fragmented and ambivalent. Employees avoid discussing conflict with teammates they see as hostile, arrogant, and closed-minded for fear of stimulating aggression and disrupting truces. They are reluctant to bring up issues with coy and passive teammates, assuming that they will withdraw from any heated discussions. These attitudes toward each other undermine confidence that employees can manage conflict openly and constructively.

As people must deal with conflict every day, they have developed skills and procedures for doing so; but individuals also develop ineffectual habits and insensitivities. Managing conflict is like skiing. On the easy slopes, it is easy to keep form and keep one's weight forward but on the steep slopes, average skiers lean back, losing control and confidence. We often let bad habits and impatience emerge when confronted with complex conflicts with people important to us. Conflict management can develop our strengths but it also reveals our weaknesses.

Avoiding Conflict

Given the significant challenges of managing conflict constructively, avoiding conflict has great appeal. Might not the conflict dissolve itself? Why take the risks of appearing to be a complainer and too emotional? Words that cannot be taken back may do irreparable damage to an already frail relationship. Might we not appear too aggressive and make our conflict partners wilt under pressure? Might they counter-attack?

We assume that we can avoid conflict by ourselves, whereas an open, cooperative approach depends also on the willingness of our colleagues to respond constructively. The benefits of avoiding conflict can be immediate as we leave the situation physically and psychologically, making avoidance very appealing. In contrast, a cooperative open approach requires effort and skill to express strong feelings and develop solutions to complex problems.

It's enticing to believe that it may not be necessary to manage conflict. Indeed, avoiding conflict is useful in some situations. It can be practical and appreciated to postpone discussing a conflict in order to find a time and situation suitable for all. Some conflicts are not worth the time and effort to be managed; people can simply agree to a solution. Avoiding conflict effectively though is not easy. For example, avoiding conflict is more constructive when people already have strong cooperative relationships (Tjosvold and Sun, 2002).

Though useful in some circumstances, avoiding conflict is ineffectual as a general way to work together. Too many organizations and teams are so preoccupied with avoiding conflict that they remain frustrated and pessimistic that they will find a reasonable way to deal with their grievances. They work to hide their feelings and conclude that their team members are too closed-minded and uncaring to discuss the issues that divide them. They are worried that even a small disagreement will boil into a war.

The reliance on avoiding conflict results in ongoing conflict. Studies indicate that the more teams rely on avoiding conflict, the more they also use competitive, win–lose ways of dealing with them. After frustration and pressure have built up in conflict avoidance, angry words are exchanged and an "I'm right, you're wrong" fight is engaged. After this win–lose approach to their conflict deepens their suspicions, they again return to avoiding. Alternating between avoiding and fighting to win very much demoralizes a team.

Conflict Management for Effective Organizations

Teams and organizations are potentially highly useful because they can combine various efforts and integrate diverse views. Why have a team if team members have similar backgrounds and think alike? The very rationale for an organization is to combine the energy, ideas, and knowledge of diverse people. But management cannot simply mix various perspectives in a bowl; people with diverse perspectives must themselves hammer out new ideas and approaches through ongoing discussion.

To work in an organization is to be in conflict. To take advantage of joint work requires conflict management. But common ideas and assumptions very much frustrate conflict management. Many leaders and team members think of conflict as a struggle against each other, as a deadly dispute where one person wins and others lose. Although they may well prefer dealing directly and helpfully with problems and differences, they assume others are committed to winning the conflict or to avoiding. These attitudes and assumptions make productive conflict difficult.

Research has identified the relationships and skills leaders and team members need to make their conflicts productive. Indeed, the book's teamwork model identifies that cooperative relationships, where team members believe that others are helping them achieve their goals as they achieve their own, are a vital foundation as they foster open-minded discussions.

Although managing conflict cooperatively demands considerable intellectual, emotional, and relational capabilities, executives, professionals, and workers have all demonstrated that they can discuss their differences openly for constructive purposes. This chapter has shown how the cooperative goals and open-minded discussion model can help team members manage their conflicts constructively. Chapter 9 describes how teams can use the model and their capabilities to deliver high quality customer service.

Action Plans

Do less of:

- Blame the conflict on someone else.
- Assume every conflict is a fight to win.
- Focus only on what you want.
- Repeat arguments in a louder voice.
- Return every slight with rebuke.
- Use "either-or," fixed pie thinking.
- Equate success with getting your way.

Do more of:

- Develop realistic attitudes that working together cooperatively requires conflict management.
- Focus on working together to discuss the conflict for win–win solutions.
- Mediate by fostering cooperative conflict management.
- Arrange a convenient time and place to discuss the conflict.
- Follow the golden rule of conflict of using the approach you want others to use: If you want others to listen to you, then listen to them.
- Put yourself in the other's shoes.
- Show respect and acceptance as you disagree.
- Define the problem together.
- Be firm in furthering mutual needs, but flexible in how to do that.
- Reach agreement or arrange more discussions.
- Celebrate your joint achievement.

III

Making the Organization a Team

Without the assistance and co-operation of many thousands, the very meanest person in a civilized country could not be provided, even according to the easy and simple manner in which he is commonly accommodated.

In civilized society [the individual] stands at all times in need of the co-operation and assistance of great multitudes, while his whole life is scarce sufficient to gain the friendship of a few persons.

Adam Smith, Wealth of Nations

9

Teamwork with Customers

"Big surprise for me," Thomas told Courtney. He kept replaying his meeting with Jeffrey, the new CFO at Donaldson on the drive back to the bank, trying to make sure he understood what happened and hoping that he did not lose the loan. He was relieved to find Courtney in her office with the door open.

"The 'Come over and meet our new CFO' invitation turned into 'Let's get a better deal for Donaldson' confrontation. The new guy wants to prove that he was the right person to hire, that they really got their money's worth when they hired him."

"Sounds like a tough meeting," Courtney said. "You don't look like you had much fun."

"He was pushing me around so that he could look good," Thomas continued. "He was being self-centered and unfair, coming in at the last moment and making such heavy demands after we have been negotiating for so long and very close to an agreement."

"Not fair, not reasonable," Courtney said.

"I wanted to say many things, fortunately I kept telling myself that we are supposed to work as a team with our customers and listen to them and try to find solutions for their needs," Thomas said. "I did a pretty good job of listening and taking notes. He liked that. I had something constructive rather than destructive to do."

"Good discipline! What does he want?" Courtney asked.

"Everything. Lower upfront fees, even lower interest rates, and he also mentioned a longer term," Thomas said. "He's not dumb. He hinted at the new national players coming into the market, suggesting that we have to be more aggressive to remain competitive. I tried to show that we are agreeable people and would consider their requests, just as we have done in the past. "

"Perhaps I should have gone with you after all," Joel said as he entered the office.

"In retrospect, yes," Thomas said. "I was caught off guard. If there were two or three of us, we could have offered more convincing counter-proposals. Now I left telling him we would consider his suggestions and get back to him soon. So another meeting."

"It's an okay outcome, maybe even the best one, given the new player there," Joel said. "Now we can brainstorm among ourselves, take some time and show them that we are considering their needs. Perhaps we should discuss with the risk management people, see the specific terms we can offer and those we cannot."

"Which risk management person? Raymond who says 'No' without a smile or Catherine who says 'No' with a smile?" Thomas asked, hoping humor would bring some relief to his morning.

Two years ago after costly experiences with several loans, the bank concentrated its risk analysis expertise into the risk management team. Raymond and Catherine often laughed that, while trained to make recommendations based on technical analyses, they were often in the middle of arguments, having to defend, deflect, and persuade. Well aware that Joel's group thought they just liked to say "No", they expected pressure and complaints.

Raymond and Catherine had worried that the Daniel's teamwork program and its emphasis on customer service would put even more pressure on them. They feared they would be on the defensive, expected to go along with the loan officers, always giving customers everything they wanted. Fortunately, Daniel had reassured them that the teamwork program meant that they should listen to the loan officers and work with them to develop loans useful for customers but they should also make sure that the loans work for the bank. He counted on them to protect the quality of the loans for the long-term health of the bank, including positive ratings from government regulators. For sure, he did not want the bank to be put on the regulators' watch list as threatened a year ago.

Daniel also reminded them to appreciate the pressures on the loans group. Upper management constantly tells them that the bank needs to sell more loans. Loan people usually want to respond to the customers' requests and to please the customers, which is basically a good thing. But the bank has to reject their proposed loan agreements on occasion. It is not easy being a loan officer, Daniel concluded.

With this background, Raymond and Catherine felt they could be straightforward with Thomas and Joel. They agreed that the terms of the loan could be changed to make it more acceptable to Donaldson. However, they conducted analyses of the options described in Thomas's memo about Donaldson's new requests. These analyses showed that any significant improvement for the customer had to be offset with an improvement for the bank. There was no easy "everyone can get a better deal" option.

Catherine explained that if they were to reduce the loan origination fees, they would just have to raise other conditions. Reducing origination fees by itself would make the loan riskier and less profitable, moving it from contributing to the bank's loan quality to undermining its quality.

> "We cannot change, is that what you're saying," Thomas said, sounding more testy than he intended. He had often heard risk management talk about loan quality.

> "We don't think that," Raymond replied calmly. "They may well value certain options more than others. We could brainstorm with you specific terms we could offer and suggest to them those that are acceptable to us."

> Catherine distributed several new loan packages that their group could support. "We thought these analyses would help us be more specific."

"You give good service," Thomas said unexpectedly, bringing smiles to everyone.

* * *

"Tough meeting with Donaldson, good meeting with risk management." Thomas summarized recent developments for Courtney.

"Teamwork with risk management is important," Courtney said. "It's a relief to think of them as allies. It's tough enough working with customers as a team without fighting with risk management."

"Working with customers is a special kind of team," Thomas said. "Customers have the power, they decide."

"The risk management people are telling us that we need a mutual, two-way relationship, the loan has to be good for the bank as well as for Donaldson," Courtney said.

"I should remember this in my meeting with Donaldson next week," Thomas said. "Let them know we want the loan to be as good for them as possible, but it has to be good for the bank too."

"The bank has to be profitable to be a long-term partner for Donaldson," Courtney said.

"When I met them last time, I tried to be agreeable," Thomas said. "Next time I will discuss differences directly, propose different options, see if we can develop an arrangement that is good for them but also good for the bank."

"That's the right attitude," Courtney said. "The specific viable options developed by risk management should also help working with Donaldson. I would like to go with you as a teammate."

"Good to have your moral and practical support," Thomas said.

Teambuilding with and for Customers

Community Bank must provide quality service to its customers or face reduced revenue and support in the future. Customers sustain an organization and without them it cannot survive. This imperative is so strong that people throughout the bank recognized it. For Joel, Thomas, and Courtney, this awareness is a daily demand. But serving customers requires developing relationships with customers, not just selling. In addition to a team organization within the bank, Community Bank needs team relationships with customers.

Like building relationships with team members, building relationships with customers only sounds easy. As Joel, Thomas, and Courtney were learning, strengthening relationships with customers is a challenge that requires the effort of both the bank and its customers. To cultivate customers requires two-way relationships where the bank is listening and responding to customers but customers are also expressing their ideas and feelings and are considering the bank's proposals and products. However, this teamwork with customers requires teamwork throughout the organization (Tjosvold, 1993). Joel, Thomas, Courtney, Catherine, and Raymond had to hammer out together mutually beneficial solutions for Donaldson.

As when building teamwork in their own marketing group, Joel, Courtney, and Thomas were learning that they needed a clear understanding of the nature of the relationship they wanted to establish with their customers. Thomas was oriented toward the customers at Donaldson, focused on understanding their needs and how the bank could meet them. He also knew that the more favorable the terms for Donaldson, the more likely he would be able to close the deal, thereby receiving recognition and a bonus. However, the risk management group reminded him very directly that teamwork is built upon cooperative, mutually beneficial relationships. The loan had to work for the bank as well as for Donaldson. He was also learning that he needed to discuss conflicts with the customers open-mindedly.

From Products to Customer Relationships

Stimulated by market demands and new technologies, companies are investing heavily in building customer relationships. They realize that with social media they can communicate with customers more intensely and effectively than ever before. Customers are also increasing their demands and expectations that companies listen and involve them. Marketing professionals are experimenting to create effective ways of using traditional and emerging media.

Companies have traditionally analyzed and focused on specific products and services. They work to develop products that appeal to customers, create marketing and advertising programs to sell these products, and continue to invest in products that are highly profitable.

Savvy firms are now moving from marketing products to cultivating customers (Rust, Moorman, and Bhalla, 2010). They are realizing that customers can be more important ingredients for long-term profitability and company success than products. Products are updated and replaced by emerging technologies and the entrance of new firms into the marketplace, making them short-term foundations for success. Recognizing that profitable customers are often a more secure basis for long-term success than profitable products, retailers have long understood that they should sell some products with no margins in order to attract customers who will buy more profitable products.

In addition, to facilitate communication from companies to customers, new technologies give customers access to more ways to register complaints, post messages, and offer suggestions. Companies like Starbucks welcome customer communications, even if they are complaints, because they signal that these customers care about the company and may well be open to becoming committed to its products, especially if the company can respond effectively to the customer's message (Merlo, Eisingerich, and Auh, 2014). Customers who do not care about the company and its products often take their business elsewhere without registering complaints, leaving the company without an opportunity to make amends.

Companies are realizing that listening to customer feedback and suggestions helps them update their products and strengthen how they relate to them. For example, Apple's Express Lane advanced support website encourages customers to describe to company technicians their reactions and frustrations with its products (Merlo et al., 2014). Apple uses these discussions to fine-tune its offerings.

Customers who communicate expect to be listened to. Companies cannot just tell and sell to customers but also need to hear and respond, perhaps especially when customers are sending complaints.

Managing Conflict with Customers

The productive team model emphasizes that companies and customers need to discuss their various ideas and grievances open-mindedly (Tjosvold and Wong, 1994; Wong and Tjosvold, 1995). Indeed, managing conflict with customers helps companies make use of customer feedback. General Mills discovered that it was undermining not strengthening its relationships with valuable partners (Avery, Fournier, and Wittenbraker, 2014). The company was listening, so it heard the outcry from customers when it tried to impose a new rule that customers who download coupons and join sweepstakes could not sue if a dispute arose. Within days, General Mills rescinded the rule, to the relief of valuable customers.

The failure to manage conflict and deal with customer complaints can be very costly to companies. Companies typically calculate their costs in responding to a complaint and making a replacement. However, customers often have a different perspective and a more extensive set of costs. They remember that the service breakdowns left them stranded, wasted their time, and made them miss meetings. With such grievances, customers think of taking their business elsewhere.

Responding to customer frustration and service breakdowns can, though, restore confidence and loyalty. A United States Office of Consumer Affairs study found that 54 per cent of the customers who suffered a service breakdown would maintain brand loyalty if their problems were resolved, but only 19 per cent would if they found the resolution unsatisfactory (Zemke and Schaaf, 1989). Customers can become more loyal after their grievances have been effectively dealt with than if they never had a complaint.

Highly successful salespeople consider customer complaints as opportunities to demonstrate their commitment to the customer, especially when the service breakdown is not their fault (Kouzes and Posner, 1995)! Then they can really show that they care for the customer. Managing conflict with customers is often challenging but can strengthen customer relationships and company long-term profitability.

Conflict management helps companies and customers fine-tune their relationships as well as company products. Customers have various preferences about how they want to communicate with companies. Based on evidence from 200 brands in 11 industries, researchers identified 29 distinct relationships that customers and companies were developing (Avery et al., 2014). Some customers want to be treated as old friends, some as close siblings, whereas other customers want to be more distanced and impersonal with companies.

Managing conflict helps companies and customers forge ways to communicate and interact that they find most rewarding. Like team relationships within a firm, productive customer relationships have cooperative goals and open-minded discussions but have various ways of actually interacting and communicating. Discussing their frustrations and diverse ideas open-mindedly can help companies and their customers shape ways to interact that are appropriate, enjoyable, and effective for both.

Customer Communities

Companies are actively encouraging customers to join together to discuss their experiences and their suggestions for the company. These communities have proved useful for strengthening the bond between companies and their products. Apple Support Communities website facilitates discussions about its products among customers (Merlo, Eisingerich, and Auh, 2014). Harley-Davidson has long profited from cohesive customer communities that reinforce loyalty to the brand. Harley employees, who are themselves committed motorcyclists, join their customers on road trips, solidifying Harley's status as a "best friend" (Avery et al., 2014). The company is a friend among a community of friends.

Customers are using technology that makes it much easier to leave comments and suggestions, but they expect companies to respond to them. Responding to substantial customer suggestions can be very costly. Companies are finding that their customer communities vet their suggestions to identify the most critical ones. Customer communities help companies focus on the frustrations and suggestions most important to customers (Rust et al., 2010).

Leaders are learning that developing teamwork among employees can motivate them and stimulate their productivity. Companies are realizing that encouraging team relationships among customers can profit both companies and their customers.

Teamwork for and with Customers

The failure to serve customers effectively is very often not a lack of individuals' interest or skill. Though managers and employees want to serve, customers end up frustrated. It takes concerted, capable, collective work for organizations to deliver value to customers.

Customers and companies have an increasing array of methods to communicate. The productive team model identifies the underlying relationships and exchanges that facilitate the effective use of these technologies for quality customer service. Companies and customers demonstrate that they have cooperative goals where they are committed to promoting each other's interests and wellbeing. Customers care about the company and its products but the company also cares about its customers. They work out disagreements and complaints for mutual benefit.

Social media and other powerful new technologies allow companies to interact with and know their customers more comprehensively and to shape their products and services more finely. But in developing team, two-way relationships of mutual benefit it is necessary for customers to use technologies to provide feedback, register complaints, and strengthen loyalty.

Action Plans

Do less of:

- Assume the present level of service is good enough.
- Believe telling employees to improve service is effective.
- Assign individuals to serve customers and blame them for service errors.
- Talk to but do not listen to customers.
- Avoid discussing customer complaints.
- Try to win arguments with customers.

Do more of:

- Focus the organization on cultivating customers.
- Form teams to serve customers.
- Develop cooperative relationships with customers.
- Trust customers so that they trust the team and company.
- Listen to as well as talk to customers.
- Consider customer complaints as valuable feedback.
- Use customer feedback to improve service.
- Manage conflicts with customers open-mindedly.
- Encourage customer communities.
- Develop teamwork with and for customers.

chapter 10

Team Organization: Departments Working Together

Believing that collaboration drives innovation and innovation drives company success. For example, Google wants employees from across the company to talk with each other (Waber, 2013). The company invests in providing physical spaces that foster employee conversations. Google New York City occupies a large single story office without physical barriers between people and groups. Its California campus encourages people to collaborate spontaneously as well as facilitate scheduled meetings. The company's physical spaces promote a community where people support each other and become friends. Google invests in helping employees feel happy to be a part of a community, and therefore more loyal and productive.

Working Together at Continental Airlines

In three years, Continental Airlines went from bankruptcy to earning awards for being the best managed airline, ranked as one of the best 100 companies in the US to work for, and rated highest among airlines for customer service. Its chief executive officer (CEO) Gordon Bethune (1999) credited its Working Together program for this turn-around.

Bethune explained that understanding that "an airline is the biggest team sport there is" led to the Working Together program. Pilots, flight attendants, gate agents, airport agents, mechanics, and reservation agents are all parts of the same "wrist-watch" that requires each and everyone to work together; the failure to understand that about the airline business means failure. To consider some people as very valuable and to demean other employees risks finding that "the watch doesn't work."

Teamwork began at Continental with top management. Bethune, the president, the chief financial officer, the head of legal and public relations, and the head of operations each brought "smarts to the table," but each could be short-sighted. "We must collectively agree or we just don't do them." When "we all say yes, it's probably OK."

On-time arrival is the most important contributor to passenger satisfaction and commitment to an airline. Continental was at the bottom of all major airlines with late arrivals costing millions of dollars in direct costs; several of these millions went to rival airlines for taking Continental passengers who had missed connections. Everyone was responsible for late planes; no one group working alone could fix the problem. The Working Together program developed a straightforward foundation to improve on-time arrivals that everyone could understand. Continental promised to deposit $65 into each employee's bank account every month the airline reached its on-time target.

The program, with each individual being rewarded when the airline reached its goal of on-time arrivals, changed how Continental employees approached poor performance. Employees stopped blaming each other and found many big and small ways to improve on-time service. If there were not enough meals on board, attendants reminded the caterer to fix the problem next time; to deal with the issue this time, attendants found passengers with whom they could trade drinks for meals so the plane could leave on time.

As its on-time arrivals improved and its customer service ratings climbed, Continental was depositing $65 checks totaling millions into employee bank accounts, rather than making deposits in those of rival airlines.

Continental invested 15 per cent of pretax income in employee profit-sharing to supplement the $65 deposits and to reinforce the message that everyone is valuable in making the "wrist-watch" of Continental work.

The Working Together program also held that as everyone has to contribute, everyone should be knowledgeable about the company. Every day Continental made sure that employees knew its stock price, on-time performance, and baggage handling errors. On Friday evenings, Bethune e-mailed everyone his perspective of the week. A monthly newsletter was sent to everyone's home and an open house was held at headquarters in Houston. Every six months, Bethune and the President gave presentations in several cities.

Bethune argued that it was not just "profit-sharing that makes people work together and feel good about going to work." Continental employees are not distracted by trying to get more benefits or other narrow interests, but "spend 100 percent of [their] time working together as a team trying to figure out how to beat competitors." To complement organization-wide monetary rewards, Bethune and other company leaders worked to develop employee professionalism. Their message convinced many employees that they were airline professionals who together deliver superior value to customers.

When he first arrived at Continental, Bethune discovered "why they were last, why they were worst—because of the dysfunctional company they were. Employees competed against each other." The airlines had "horrible labor relations" that resulted in poor product delivery. "I've never heard of a successful company that didn't have people who liked working there. Sooner or later, you've got to make peace with the employees and have people who actually like going to work."

Demands for Specialists to Work Together

In airlines and many organizations, specialists are asked to work with each other and clients. Finance and accounting departments are moving away from their roles as controllers and "policemen" to those who help operating specialists solve problems. At Merck, according to the CFO, Judy Lewent, finance specialists "work with a very sharp pencil. We are not lax" (Nichols, 1994). But they also "attempt to work with the operating units and, in many cases, have been accepted as a partner in the business." Instead of maintaining that a new agricultural product was too expensive to meet revenue targets, they worked with those committed to the product to uncover that the packaging was adding too much cost. They fulfilled their mandate of protecting Merck's financial resources but also helped operating specialists make their business viable.

Cross-functional teamwork should not weaken professional identity. Indeed, professionals may be grouped by discipline so that they can update their knowledge. Profitable, high return pharmaceutical companies encourage their researchers to keep active within their disciplines in and out of the company through conferences, joint projects, and publications (Henderson, 1994). These companies also make sure that their specialists interact with each other and with product and marketing specialists. They discuss each other's projects and debate which ones can be profitably developed.

Many specialists become demoralized trying to work across functional and organizational boundaries. They feel on opposite sides, unable to solve problems. It is not just the complexity of creative problem solving that impedes cross-functional teamwork. They often fail to build the relationships where they value each other's specialty and feel united so that they can discuss their views directly and integrate them. Cooperative goals and open-minded discussion are needed for productive exchange as specialists work across boundaries.

Challenges to Strengthen Cooperative Goals between Departments

With examples such as Bethune at Continental, organizational leaders increasingly appreciate the costs of competition and the value of coordination between departments and other units. However, just because leaders want coordination does not mean that it happens. Indeed, many leaders are ambivalent about cooperation and competition and send mixed messages.

Leaders, even those who talk about the importance of cooperation, may also believe that competition within organizations is useful. They assume it will foster lively debate and create new ideas as well as motivate. Competitive rivalry is thought not only inevitable but also a stimulus to productivity. Competition between departments is expected to build cooperation within departments as departments coalesce around outdoing each other, mirroring the free market of competition between companies.

Many leaders talk about "winners and losers." They devise reward systems such as ranking units from top to bottom that they believe will motivate units to achieve at high levels as they debate who has the best ideas and work to implement them.

These leaders give mixed messages to the groups within the organization. They want the groups to work together but they often encourage and reward competition. But, as the next section argues, competition under-mines open-minded discussions, disrupts coordination between groups, and fails to stimulate group productivity.

In addition to mixed messages from leaders, developing cooperative goals and effective coordination between departments presents practical challenges. As argued in Chapter 4, small teams help members get to know each other as individuals and combine each other's abilities. But it is difficult for individuals to know each other across large, diverse organiza-tions. Organizations and even departments can often be spread out across buildings, cities, even countries. How can large, dispersed units be "knee-to-knee and eye-to-eye" to facilitate communication and understanding? How can they develop common tasks so that they can see that their goals are cooperative?

Discussing conflict productively can be especially difficult across depart-ments. Gossiping and complaining about other departments is a tradition in many companies. However, departments do not schedule meetings nor develop the confidence to discuss conflicts directly with each other. Rather than use their frustrations to develop more effective coordination, they let their conflicts divide them.

Leaders need a clear appreciation of the value of cooperative goals and have effective strategies to develop them. The next section reviews studies that document the value of cooperative goals between departments and specialists and how competition can very much frustrate effective organizational work. A later section identifies strategies that convince organizational leaders and specialists that their goals are cooperative.

CONSTRUCTIVE COMPETITION

Competition is prevalent and widespread in most societies; excellence is often defined in terms of out-performing others. Competition is celebrated as a great motivator for individuals and groups. The free market system is thought superior to centrally controlled economies because its competition stimulates companies to innovate.

A roadblock to assessing the contribution of competition to performance is the various definitions of competition. Competition is defined as having high standards, high aspirations, or even high performance itself. Having people use the same word to mean different things causes confusion. Deutsch's theory (1949) defines competition as negatively related, "win–lose" goals that allow clear comparisons with cooperation as positively related, mutual goals.

Competition between groups has long been thought to promote team productivity. Team members are thought to pull together and work hard to outdo other teams. This competition is expected to strengthen coordination within teams, though it may undermine coordination between teams. Team sports are common examples.

Studies confirm that competition can be constructive. In experiments, people completed tasks that required quick responses and where the time and effort to coordinate would not much improve but would slow responses (Beersman, Hollenbeck, Humphrey, Moon, Colon, and Ilgen, 2003). Competition has also been found to motivate children to move marbles from one side of a classroom to the other.

However, meta-analyses findings of studies do not support the common belief that intergroup competition stimulates group productivity. Cooperation between teams, compared to competition between them, was found to strengthen team productivity (Johnson and Johnson, 2005). In most situations, teams are more effective when they coordinate and support each other rather than when they try to undo each other. No study we know has shown competition to stimulate greater performance than cooperation on difficult tasks in actual organizations. Findings underscore the limited utility and potential considerable damage that organizational leaders can have when they encourage competition between teams.

Why should competition offer such limited value to organizations? Whereas cooperative goals promote efforts to assist each other and open-minded discussion to develop effective solutions, competition frustrates mutual assistance, leaving people and teams to cope on their own. Typically in organizations, teams need information and knowledge from other teams to be productive but competition undercuts teams' willingness to assist, as they want to outdo, not lose to other teams. Cooperative goals develop social support and relationships, both of which promote a wide range of positive outcomes in organizations, including performance.

Recognizing it fares poorly compared to cooperation in most situations, researchers have tried to document when competition is constructive. Employees described specific incidents of productive competition and then rated motives, conditions, and strategies used in the competition (Tjosvold, Johnson, Johnson, and Sun, 2003; Tjosvold, Johnson, and Sun, 2006). Fair rules of how to compete and who will win, strong prior relationships, and an internal desire to compete contributed to making competition constructive. Managerial and other external pressures to compete did not. Individuals and groups should also believe that they have a reasonable chance to win the competition; they have little reason to work hard to win if they believe it's impossible for them to do so.

Results, taken together, underline that developing conditions for constructive competition is difficult. Developing fair rules that convince everyone they can "win" is typically challenging, often impossible. Strong prior relationships can contribute to making competition constructive but cooperation promotes strong relationships. Making competition constructive in organizations is much more difficult than making cooperation constructive.

Research on Specialists Working Together

Evidence from surveys, experiments, and case studies support the foundations of Continental's Working Together program. Moving away from competition toward establishing strong cooperative links between diverse teams very much contributes to open-minded communication between departments that in turn solves problems and promotes effective organizational work.

Hospitals are among the most disciplinary fragmented of all organizations; just the medical staff is divided into specialties, sub-specialties, and sub-sub specialties. They confront increasing pressures and demands to use resources more efficiently to sustain and improve the quality of care. Physicians are a prime driver of health care costs and it seems evident that they must be involved, but having physicians and administrators on the same committee is insufficient.

Interviews with physicians and nursing administrators indicated that when they discussed their differences openly and constructively they solved hospital problems that promoted both the quality of care and reduced costs (Tjosvold and MacPearson, 1996). Through open-minded discussion, physicians and nursing administrators felt positive about their collaboration, strengthened their work relationships, made progress on the task, contributed to the effectiveness of the hospital, used resources efficiently, built their confidence in future problem solving, and fostered quality care Competitive, closed discussion of ideas disrupted their relationships and work and contributed little to patients or the hospital. Similar to results at Continental, developing cooperative goals very much helped the hospital professionals discuss issues open-mindedly to improve quality, affordable health care.

Analyses of cases of collaboration between accounting professionals and managers also confirm the teamwork model. Specifically, accounting professionals and managers solved shortcomings and resolved misunderstandings to realize the potential of new control and information systems to generate timely, useful information (Poon, Pike, and Tjosvold, 2001; Tjosvold and Poon, 1998a, 1998b). Accountants and line managers who had cooperative goals discussed opposing views open-mindedly and made their accounting systems operate effectively. Managers became more appreciative of the accounting procedures, more understanding of their rationale, and convinced of their importance; they were also more confident they could work together with accountants in the future.

Many studies support that the effects of cooperation and competition found within a group also occur between groups, supporting that the value of cooperative goals and open-minded discussion applies between departments as well as between teammates. For example, 125 CEOs and 436 executives from 125 companies were surveyed on the relationships and interactions among their departments. Results showed that cooperative, but not competitive and independent, goals along with shared rewards helped departments feel psychologically safe and thus able to discuss their experiences openly, including how to learn from mistakes (Chen and Tjosvold, 2012). Studies have documented the significant contribution of cooperative goals among top management team members to effective strategic leadership of organizations (Chen and Tjosvold, 2008, 2012; Chen, Tjosvold, and Liu, 2006; Chen, Liu, and Tjosvold, 2005).

Competition between departments may be useful in some situations; having departments compete for who has the best bowling team, can raise the most for a charity, or win a tug of war can add fun and excitement and help people get to know each other. However, serious competitive rivalry between departments undermines coordination and problem solving. Professionals, managers, and other specialists from different departments focused on their cooperative goals should discuss their various views open-mindedly so that they integrate their ideas and efforts to make their organizations effective for their customers and for themselves.

Strengthening Cooperative Goals between Departments

Cooperative goals between departments powerfully promote coordination between departments that helps them to integrate their ideas and resources. This section shows how managers and employees can use shared vision, community, and joint rewards to strengthen their organization's cooperative goals.

Shared Vision

A shared vision helps employees throughout the organization to understand that by working together they can achieve meaningful goals. They recognize that they can accomplish tasks, reach goals, and make a difference that they could not do alone.

Our family business provides residential services for persons with special needs so that they can develop themselves as they live and work in the community. Employees realize that they can very much contribute to the lives of our clients as well as make communities more compassionate and inclusive. We enhance this shared vision by involving employees in promoting the lives and wellbeing of people around the world. As mentioned earlier, they raise money, send supplies, and make visits to give lessons at an elementary school in Cameroon that educates 200 children who would otherwise have no education.

Making profits can be meaningful; we want our family business to have the discipline to make profits. Profits indicate that the organization has used its resources wisely. It has created greater value for customers, as measured by how much customers are willing to pay for its products, than the resources the company had to use to create them. Making profits also provides assurance that employees will continue in their jobs and contribute to the wellbeing and lives of their families and communities.

Measures of the organization's success reinforce meaningful goals in that employees can see that they are making a difference. Keeping records of our clients' progress in becoming more independent convinces them and staff members that they are achieving their goals. For profit-making companies, rising profits and share prices provide concrete evidence of their joint success.

Community

Organization members feel united if they believe they belong to one community; they identify with their organization and feel they are at one with it (Carmeli, Gilat, and Waldman, 2007; Haslam, Jettern, Postmes, and Haslam, 2009; Lee, Farth, and Chen, 2011). Being valued members of a worthy community strengthens self-concepts. As they make their organization better, managers and employees strengthen their own self-esteem. The more employees identify with the organization, the more willing they are to follow its norms and promote its values. Organizational identification increases loyalty, job performance, commitment, and reduces turnover intentions.

A meaningful community fosters a "caring culture." People identify and commit themselves to companies in which they feel accepted, valued, and supported (Rhoades and Eisenberger, 2002). Organizations show they care about individuals by responding to their special needs, celebrating their birthdays and personal victories, and supporting them in crises. Employees also know that the organization cares for its stakeholders and customers by providing quality service, good value, and effective responses to complaints.

Companies identify values that they believe in and that support their shared vision. Many employees accept Whole Foods Market values to provide natural, organic foods (Lagace, 2003). They are not just selling food and building a sound business model; they are changing the world and improving the quality of lives of their customers. These values make employees' work more meaningful and emphasize that employees belong together and are helpful "citizens" to each other and their customers.

Norms are typically implicit expectations about how people are expected to interact and treat each other. As suggested in Chapter 4, organizations can make them explicit by together identifying the ways of working together that will enhance them, the organization, and their customers.

Companies are also developing campuses that turn physical proximity into psychological unity. In addition to having their offices close to each other, employees share open spaces, cafeterias, and exercise facilities. To supplement informal interaction, organizations hold regular meetings and exchanges where people meet each other as individuals, learn about developments throughout the organization, and celebrate each other's successes.

Many organizations invest in developing logos, company songs, and other symbols of their identity. These symbols can help employees feel part of a community.

Shared Rewards

Distributing the benefits of organizational work widely and fairly reinforces organizational cooperative goals and feelings of community. People understand that their own individual rewards depend upon the progress of the organization. If the company succeeds, then everyone will receive tangible and intangible benefits. Our family business distributes coupons redeemable for merchandise for individual and team contributions.

Although there is much attention on the impact of distributing money and other tangible benefits, the distribution of intangible rewards like appreciation can also be very constructive. Thank you notes, birthday cards, write-ups in the company newsletter, and identifying achievements in meetings all reward and reinforce teams to continue to contribute. Employees find certificates recognizing their years of service to the organization and its customers meaningful. Leaders catch employees doing good things and let them know they and the organization appreciate their contributions.

Many organizations could distribute recognition much more widely and generously. Public recognition communicates to employees that they have contributed effort to the organization and are valued. There is no scarcity of appreciation; it should be given genuinely, generously, and frequently.

Sharing rewards widely strengthens cooperative goals, but that does not mean distributing the same rewards is required, or even desirable. Every person is different and contributes in different ways. Surely, intangible rewards like recognition depend on the individual and group. Equally and fairly do not mean identically.

However, if top management or other groups claim a very large part of the profits, recognition, and other benefits earned by the organization, the danger is that others will doubt that goals are really cooperative and that they actually belong to one effort and community. They may conclude that these "superior" groups are exploiting them. Some win, they lose; people are "not in this together."

Relatively equal rather than heavily unequal distributions of rewards are most reinforcing of cooperative goals and community. Some inequality people are willing to accept and believe fair. Highly significant unequal rewards considered an injustice disrupt cooperative effort whereas relatively equal rewards thought fair strengthen organizational unity.

Distributing Rewards at Community Bank

"It's only money, I kept thinking, what's the big deal about it?" Daniel said. He was recounting for his Leadership Development Team (LDT) the furor at the last management meeting on ways to reward teamwork throughout the company. He had proposed depositing the same amount of money for each employee every month that the bank meets its goals. "What could be more concrete and motivating than this common bonus? It communicates that everyone can and should contribute to the bank and, when they do, the bank succeeds and individuals are rewarded. Teamwork written big."

Naomi said, "It's simple, powerful, direct. I like it."

"It puts the power of rewards behind teamwork between departments," Serge said.

Daniel had strong feelings to express. "We talk but do little to encourage teamwork across departments. Most departments do their own thing, more interested in blaming 'the other guys' than working together."

"Tensions between departments are common, they are still annoying," Serge said.

"Managers had many worries about the plan," Daniel said. "How can we be sure that our measures of the bank's success are accurate, how will stockholders react to giving away money, the bonus is not fair because some people do not contribute directly to the bank's profits, some people do much more for the bank but everyone gets the same, the bonus will cause contention not harmony."

"Many people, especially higher up the organization, are change negative; they'll do anything to keep things as they are," Naomi said.

Leslie argued that the managers raised good points that deserve consideration. Just because we might think the plan is obviously useful, that does not mean that employees do or that it is effective. Many projects designed to unite people ended up dividing them. Employees should believe that the program is fair as well as effective; they are the ones that have to make the plan work. They should feel confident that the program will help them be more productive as well feel more enhanced. That way, employees will use the program to help the company and themselves. Being forced to accept a new program and feeling unjustly treated undermine employee unity, commitment, and productivity.

Naomi thought getting everyone to agree on what is fair is an impossible dream. Serge pointed out that his kids fight over what is fair everyday all day.

Leslie agreed people have their own ideas of what is fair as well as what is effective. But managers should still try to make good use of resistance to change, not simply overcome it. They should encourage employees to express their ideas and skepticism and try to use this dissent constructively. Open-mindedly discussing opposing views can improve the quality of decisions about the program.

Open-minded discussion is also a powerful, practical way to help people become convinced that a new program is fair as well as effective. Through controversy, they can better understand the program's rationale and have their objections recognized. They are more likely to consider the program fair and balanced as various opinions and objections have challenged it and were used to revise and improve the program.

Employee participation is very useful for managing change in organizations. But this participation has to be open and lively where dissent is welcome and opposing ideas are discussed.

Daniel explained that he had read about where a CEO developed the plan of depositing equal amounts in everyone's paycheck. It seemed that if it worked there, it could work at the bank. He was really surprised by the resistance.

> "Bonuses are a big deal," Naomi said. "It's not just about money, it's about what money means. 'I get a big bonus, I've done a lot, I'm successful, I'm competent.'"
>
> "If I get a low or no bonus, I'm a failure, incompetent," Serge added.
>
> "Everyone would get the same," Daniel defended. "There's beauty in that."
>
> "Agree, but some people find that a radical, unwelcomed, and even unfair message," Leslie said. "They think they're more important than others."

"People should not think like that," Daniel said. "Everyone's important."

"That's easier for the bank president to believe; everyone knows that you're important," Naomi said. "Some people believe that they should try to be better than others."

"These are reasons why you need participation and debate about team rewards for the bank," Leslie said. "You want to be able to respond to people's concerns, show them that you are trying to be fair, that you want everyone to feel fairly treated."

Leslie continued that equal rewards are useful, but we shouldn't think of equality too literally. People are different; they contribute differently to the organization. It's not realistic to treat them all the same. Everyone is recognized and considered important but that does not mean that they have to be treated and rewarded identically.

"You are saying that equal treatment and rewards need not be identical," Daniel said. "I have to think about that."

"It's one reason you need discussion so that people can see that they're fairly treated though not identically," Leslie said. "Like many important issues, developing team incentives and bonuses is an important task that requires a team."

"I jumped to the conclusion that depositing the same amount of money would be a good, quick solution," Daniel said.

"It may work very well for one company, but the same plan may not work for others," Leslie said.

"I still want to do something," Daniel said.

"Good," Serge said. "Getting people across our organizations working together would contribute to everyone, including customers."

"People in my company will talk to each other if I call a meeting," Naomi said. "It would be better if they find ways to help each other without me."

Leslie argued that a collaborative culture is possible but managers must build camaraderie and exchange. Chapter 10 in the book the team is reading has a section on developing cooperative goals for departments in one organization. She asked each person to read the section and then discuss it with the person next to him or her to help each other understand how to build cooperative goals for departments. These pairs should also brainstorm how Daniel can strengthen cooperative goals across the bank's departments.

After 15 minutes of reading and discussing in pairs, Leslie asked them what they had learned.

> "I notice the headings," Serge said. "I learned that trick in a speed reading course! Seriously, it's useful to realize that organizational goals, community, and shared rewards can work together to develop a team organization. We don't have to rely on one golden stroke but have several approaches."

> "One golden stroke might not work well," Naomi said. "My friend said his company profit sharing has had little impact on company performance despite high expectations."

Leslie summarized evidence indicating that rewarding employees based on company profits is not enough to improve company performance. Employees also need to have practical ways that they can contribute to improving company performance. Profit-sharing plans are more effective when employees actively identify issues and develop specific ways to promote organization performance.

Team members discussed how they could apply the ideas they had just read. They began to see that, though no quick fix, they had powerful ways to strengthen cooperative company goals.

Leslie suggested that Daniel form a task force to consider ways to help departments work together. Developing organization-wide rewards and coordination is a complex task that all departments should understand and accept. A diverse task force is needed to develop a collaborative culture. Daniel should select people from various departments, help them get to know each other as individuals, arrange sessions so that they can be knee-to-knee, eye-to-eye, and assign them common tasks to develop organization-wide rewards that promote coordination. Like other teams, it can use the teamwork model of cooperative goals and open-minded discussion as a guide to strengthen their teamwork.

The LDT group discussed how to solve the problem of involving all the departments but keeping the task force small and manageable. The bank's practice is to have a representative from each department. This may be "fair" but it led to long, inefficient meetings with unequal involvement. Daniel liked abandoning the "fair through large numbers" idea and asking task force members to confer with people throughout the organization. They are agents of the organization, not just their department.

The group discussion helped specify plans. Daniel should charge the task force to develop its principles and propose at least three ways that the bank could encourage and reduce obstacles to teamwork across the departments.

Leslie offered to help Daniel find a student who could search the research and professional literatures on shared rewards and team incentives to help the task force's deliberations. The goal was to find viable, effective, and fair ways to encourage and reward coordination throughout the bank that people understood and accepted.

> "The task force shouldn't think it needs to find the ultimate solution," Leslie said. "Just step-by-step. Plan, try, assess, modify."

> "It takes a lot of collaboration to develop organization-wide coordination," Naomi said.

> "It's a challenge," Leslie agreed. "The method reinforces the message: You're using teamwork across the departments to develop a team organization."

> "Sounds a little odd, but there's logic," Serge said.

> "The task force should propose how their plans would strengthen cooperative goals and open-minded discussion," Leslie said. "Their suggestions might surprise us."

Action Plans

Do less of:

- Assume professionals have to be generalists to work together.
- Allow departments to avoid conflicts.
- Hope that collaboration among departments will naturally occur.
- Conclude that rivalries between departments are inevitable.
- Believe that competition fosters lively, productive dialogue.

Do more of:

- Strengthen the professional expertise of all members.
- Place specialists with independent views in cross-functional teams to solve important problems.
- Develop a shared vision for specialists and departments to believe that by working together they can accomplish important goals.
- Strengthen a sense of community so that specialists feel united.
- Discuss how specialists and departments share values and care for each other.
- Have specialists work face-to-face and get to know each other.
- Have specialists declare they will support each other.
- Develop norms for departments to work together.
- Discuss what is a fair distribution of rewards that will strengthen company unity.
- Reward all departments fairly when the company succeeds.
- Have departments compete on minor issues that everyone enjoys, even if they lose.

chapter 11

Partnering with Competitors and Government: Moving to the Team Economy

We make the best decisions when we talk to people who know things we don't and understand things differently. If NGOs, businesses, and governments can work together creatively, we can help all the world's people live in dignity. We can all be effective global citizens.

Bill Clinton, 42nd US President

[Government leaders] do not realize that the corporate goal of profit maximization at all costs does not serve the interests of the nation. They do not realize that the fundamental goals of the country and of our companies have diverged. The sole focus on profit maximization, which leads to off shoring and holds down wages, does not serve the nation. We must act to realign the goals of company and country.

Ralph Gomory (2010)
Former IBM executive and Sloan Foundation President

Joel explained that Margaret from Mountain Bank had called him last month proposing to be partners in developing pork for export industry in the area. He knows her from a course they had taken a year ago.

"Mountain Bank wants to help us get more customers, that's interesting and appealing," Thomas said as the loan office team prepared to meet with people from Mountain Bank.

"It's the crazy world we live in," Courtney said. "One day we worry that they will grab our customers from us, the next day we discuss their proposal we go into business together."

Soon Margaret and Paul from Mountain Bank joined the meeting and introduced themselves.

"We want to be your partner!" Margaret said.

"I'm suspicious already," Joel replied.

Everyone laughed.

Margaret explained that East West Foods had told Mountain Bank that their customers in China are intent on sourcing pork supplies internationally. Chinese farmers could not meet the growing demand for high quality pork that increasingly prosperous customers wanted. Farmers could not produce enough quality feed nor develop sufficient environmentally friendly environments for raising pigs that the Chinese now require. An important solution was to import quality pork from the West. East West Foods was convinced that this would become a genuine market and they wanted to participate in it.

East West Foods and Mountain Bank had worked earlier on a project to market vitamin-rich rice production. Mountain Bank provided loans and financial support to feed companies, farmers, and logistic companies that expanded their facilities in order to grow and deliver the rice. Mountain Bank was happy to participate in the program, benefiting from higher sales growth and gaining more experience in emerging markets.

The bank also learned that its participation was very demanding. The bank was unprepared to process and manage many small and medium sized loans efficiently. They had to work hard to get local people to trust them and to complete bank risk analyses on many new customers. Doing things that they were not very good at, they were distracted from exploring new businesses. For the pork venture, they wanted a bank partner that local farmers and officials knew and felt comfortable with. This partner should also have the physical location and capabilities to process and manage small and medium sized loans efficiently.

> "We are focused on taking the lead in developing programs for emerging international market opportunities," Paul said. "We think we're good at this, can develop our bank around it, and do some good for the country and our trading partners. We're optimistic that we can develop the right capabilities to operate in promising markets. The more we specialize and focus though, the more we need partners."

Margaret proposed that the partnership would allow both banks to do what they are good at. Mountain Bank would concentrate on developing large loans to big feed and processing plants and Community Bank would handle smaller loans to farm producers and local feed plants. East West Foods would handle the marketing and logistics getting the pork into China and selling it to distributors.

> "I see your logic," Thomas said.
>
> "We have many good local relationships and loan processing capabilities, we aren't too comfortable handling big loans alone," Courtney said. "Good choice calling us."
>
> "Our president has plans," Joel explained. "We're mandated to grow our loan portfolio. Our processing capabilities could be made better use of and expanded. We may just need you!"
>
> "Glad to hear that you understand how the partnership could be useful for both of us," Margaret said. "We've learned, though, that understanding is the easy part. Making the partnership work is much harder. We have to get to know each other, find concrete ways to coordinate, iron out disputes, and so on. It's more difficult than it sounds."
>
> "Daniel wants us to work as a team; it's a good idea but also much more challenging than it sounds," Joel said.
>
> "We're told that teamwork is the more for more solution, you have to give more before you get more," Thomas said. "Now we're starting to believe that teamwork is not easy, not free."

"Partnerships would be similar," Joel said.

"It's good you are working on teamwork," Paul said. "The last thing we need is a disorganized partner. One person tells you one thing, another tells you something else. One person gives a commitment but it seems no one else in the company even heard it. Very frustrating for us."

"One reason I called Joel was because I had heard about your teamwork program," Margaret said. "It's hard enough to work between organizations without one partner being disorganized."

"We have made some progress working as a team," Thomas said. "We don't want to set your expectations too high!"

"Some of the things we're learning we can apply to developing our partnership," Joel said.

"Good idea!" Margaret said.

Margaret suggested that she develop a draft of an understanding about the partnership and then work with Joel to revise it. This draft would be preliminary and conceptual. The document could help their bosses and others get oriented toward the partnership. Now they should look for approval from their presidents to consider the partnership. After approvals, they could draw up a business plan.

Joel knew what he should do next: Discuss with the risk management group to understand their thinking about providing loans to farmers and small and medium sized companies in the pork supply chain. He did not want to surprise Raymond and Catherine with a developed business plan with Mountain Bank; he wanted to give them time to consider and research the project. As his team would be working with the risk management team in order to make specific loan offers, it made sense to work with them first to develop the overall program. Joel would take the step-by-step, team approach to developing this business, an approach that could pay off in the long term.

Joel also expected that Daniel would immediately want to know the risk management group's thoughts on the Mountain Bank partnership. Daniel saw risk management as a critical resource to help the bank develop stronger foundations for loan offers. He wanted to be convinced, and he wanted regulators to be convinced, that the bank's loans were reasonable. The bank should be more adventuresome—not simply give loans to people they know in traditional businesses. However, he wanted the bank also to be cautious and analytical. He saw the risk management group as contributing very much to this vision.

Somewhat surprising to Joel, Raymond and Catherine seemed eager to consider the new program. As a child, Raymond often visited his cousins' dairy farm, staying for a week or two in the summer. Catherine knew little about local farming but was eager to learn. Both were interested in China and understanding Chinese markets. They would though need time to study and learn. Joel assured them that Mountain Bank wanted to move forward but recognized that this was a long-term program and there was no pressing deadline. No customer was waiting for an answer.

They agreed that the Mountain Bank partnership had the potential to contribute to the whole bank as well as to make their own work more interesting. Joel would next help Margaret develop the preliminary overview and discuss with Daniel.

Joel was not surprised that Daniel was happy about the possible partnership with Mountain Bank as it promoted several parts of his vision for Community Bank. Daniel had already begun to consider developing partnerships with other banks. The old way of trying to do everything oneself is not cost efficient; going it alone meant missing opportunities. Competitors could become partners where they both win.

> "It sounds strange to cooperate with your competitors, but it isn't," Daniel said.
>
> "It's even popular," Joel responded.
>
> "Business people have seen concrete opportunities and begun partnerships with competitors despite the thinking that the free market system depends upon competition," Daniel said. "Sometimes we have to challenge outmoded ideas like competition is the foundation of an effective economy."

"We'll still have real competitors," Joel said.

"Sure, but having people work together throughout an industry and with government officials is even more difficult than getting people to work together in an organization," Daniel said. "We know how to compete with competitors but cooperating with them is challenging. As will be working with Mountain Bank."

"Exciting too," Joel said.

"I'm happy to know that the risk management people are already involved," Daniel said. "We need to know what we are getting ourselves into. If we're going to be innovative, we also have to be realistic and careful in developing our positions. We do not want to innovate the wrong way!"

"How about we develop a controversy so that people throughout the bank become more knowledgeable about the partnership and understand why we should or should not pursue it," Daniel continued. "By debating the pros and cons of this partnership, everyone can learn and express what they hope will happen as well as what they fear might happen."

Daniel had another point to make: "This is an interesting view of leadership. Leaders do not simply make decisions, but encourage open discussion so that the group makes good decisions."

"Subtle difference, but a big difference too," Joel said.

"Leaders have to learn a whole new set of skills and strategies if they are going to really work with and through employees to make decisions," Daniel said. "This is what our LDT is about."

After reading a preliminary outline of the partnership, Daniel asked every department to consider whether and how the bank should pursue the partnership. Together the bank should identify major success factors as well as conditions that would frustrate progress. The operations, market research, and risk management groups developed short position papers about the proposed partnership where they summarize their research and opinions.

Daniel wanted to experiment with structuring controversy to promote discussion throughout the bank. Joel thought that it might be too early to make a final decision and that should involve the board as well as other top managers. Daniel agreed that the board would have to be involved. However, the structured controversy would get many people thinking, discussing, and learning. Formal decisions would come later.

A week later, Daniel welcomed departments to the meeting. He reminded them that he believed that if they were going to make a change and do something different, then it was important that the change be potentially highly beneficial.

> "We're all already busy, we're not looking to keep busy, but we're looking to get stronger and more effective," Daniel said. "We're here today to discuss whether and how the partnership with Mountain Bank can help us be more successful for ourselves and for our community. We also want to anticipate pitfalls that could frustrate us."

> "As discussed before," Gregory said. "A new venture should not just help a little bit but help us a lot. If we're going to do something demanding, it should have a big upside."

> "And the benefits should be probable, not just theoretically possible!" Daniel said.

> He thanked operations, marketing research, and risk management for developing background papers and hoped that everyone had a chance to study them. "Let's all thank them," as he led a round of applause.

> "We should thank them especially for keeping the reports short!" James from operations said to general agreement and more applause.

Then Daniel explained why they were asked to sit in assigned seats, identified with their names on the back of the chair. The chairs were placed into groups of four to form their workshop group where they would discuss knee-to-knee and eye-to-eye, specifically debating the pros and cons of the partnership. Joel then explained that they selected people for these groups to maximize diversity and give people the opportunity to work with those they typically do not.

Employees first should make sure they know the names and education backgrounds of each person in their group of four; then they should find out each other's favorite way to manage stress and why. The groups had five minutes to discuss these items.

Then Joel explained that they would practice basic steps of open-minded discussion, namely, prepare and present their position, listen to and demonstrate that they understand the opposing position, integrate the best ideas and reasoning from both sides, and then agree to a mutually beneficial solution. He would lead them step-by-step.

Daniel explained that this structured approach allowed them to focus on and practice the basic aspects of discussing controversy open-mindedly. "It may feel a bit unusual, but it's a good way to learn."

Joel told them that the two people in front of the each group of four had the position that the bank should form the partnership and the two in the back the position that the bank should not. The pairs should now move their chairs so that they are sitting knee-to-knee with their partner assigned the same position. The pair should together develop all the arguments they can that support their assigned position. Each person should keep a list of their arguments because each person would be arguing their assigned position with a person in their next pair.

After eight minutes, Daniel asked them to thank their partner for helping them get prepared. Now the two persons on the right and two persons on the left should move their chairs to sit knee-to-knee in new pairs. The pro-partnership person should begin by presenting his or her opening position, followed by the con person's opening position. Then the two of them should debate their ideas openly and forcefully to help the other person understand and appreciate their position. Each of them should find weaknesses in the other's arguments and develop more arguments that support their assigned position.

After ten minutes, Joel told them to move to the next part of open-minded discussion: Demonstrate that they understand the opposing views. Each person should restate in her own words the other's major arguments; that is, the pro person should summarize the con's position, the con person should summarize the pro's position.

Then the pairs should combine their best ideas to summarize their findings about the partnership that both sides support. Next they should make tentative conclusions about whether and how Community Bank should develop the partnership with Mountain Bank.

Five minutes later, Joel asked them to reform their group of four to compare the ideas and conclusions of each pair and keep a record of their major conclusions on their group's "Findings Sheet." Each group of four should report at least two of their major ideas and conclusions about the partnership. These reporting sheets would be later compiled and the summaries would be distributed to give each person a written record of everyone's findings.

Daniel asked groups to volunteer to present one of their major findings. Groups recognized that the partnership could help the bank expand and develop its business and the risks seemed manageable, but they also wondered whether the bank's departments had the resources needed to serve additional customers. Groups were concerned that bank employees had the time and skills needed to develop the partnership so that they actually worked together productively with Mountain Bank.

> "Good ideas," Daniel said in summary. "I think we're saying that we can proceed with the partnership but we should have our eyes open to make sure the partnership pays off. We must be willing to invest in developing our work relationships with Mountain Bank."
>
> Joel added, "As mentioned by several groups, we can use our understanding and work at teambuilding to develop our relationship with Mountain Bank. Margaret told us that one reason they approached us is because they knew we were developing our teamwork."
>
> "I want to emphasize that we should try to understand Mountain Bank's culture and ways of working," Daniel said. "We'll have to adjust to them as they will to us."
>
> "One group wondered how Mountain Bank plans to deal with bank regulators worried about industrial collusion and anti-competition practices," Joel said. "Margaret said that they're proactive in discussing with the government rather than hoping the government won't notice and

then trying to manage crises when the government finds out. We should learn to be more proactive with regulators."

Daniel nodded in agreement, saying he wanted the bank to develop better relationships with bank regulators. He added, "We want to contribute to developing a new industry and new opportunities for the community, we are adding value and have no reason to hide from regulators."

Daniel indicated that he appreciated how everyone took the controversy seriously; he could see them working to learn more about the partnership and considering what would be best for the bank. This experience further convinced him that he should try to be an effective leader by fostering open discussion and common conclusions, not by imposing his decisions.

To reflect on the session, Joel asked the groups of four to identify three ways that they liked about how their group discussed with each other and at least one way they could improve. Then he asked group members to thank each other for helping each other discuss open-mindedly and learn about the partnership.

Daniel and Joel were upbeat as they brought the meeting to a close. They hoped that this experience would reinforce that discussions at the bank should be open-minded. Certainly there would be many issues to identify and resolve as they decided whether and how to partner with Mountain Bank. They thanked the employees for participating fully in the controversy.

Teambuilding Inside for Teamwork Outside

Teambuilding within Community Bank was reaping benefits for its partnership with Mountain Bank. Joel had quickly involved Raymond and Catherine as well as his team colleagues to consider and develop a partnership with Mountain Bank. He expected that they would have valuable opinions and ideas to improve the proposed joint venture; he could count on them to consider the partnership fully and fairly. Raymond and Catherine felt respected and saw doing research on the proposal as another way for them to enrich their work and be valued within the bank.

Joel also felt empowered because he expected that Daniel wanted him to show leadership by getting people involved and have an open-minded discussion throughout the bank. Daniel did not want Joel or himself to dominate decision making; he wanted to involve people to develop the best decision possible for the bank. These discussions would help employees appreciate the reasoning behind the ultimate decision.

The bank's teambuilding work helped prepare employees for making the structured controversy session successful. Bank employees looked forward to participating rather than watching a small minority dominate the meeting. They understood that Daniel and Joel were trying to help them discuss the partnership open-mindedly. They took advantage of the structured controversy to dig into the partnership question and develop their thinking about it.

The session also helped Daniel and Joel show that they were together leading the bank's consideration of the partnership. Leaders should demonstrate teamwork as well as espouse it.

TEAM ALLIANCES TO COPE WITH CLIMATE CHANGE

Rising sea levels is a dramatic, potentially highly destructive consequence of climate change. Hurricane Sandy's awesome power and damage brought this reality home to the US northeast coast in 2012. Communities and government officials began to consult the Netherlands with its centuries of experience living below sea levels and dealing with high sea levels (Shorto, 2014).

Henk Ovink, a Dutch water-management expert, was dismayed at the individualistic approach to dealing with water he observed on the US northeast coast. Communities thought locally: What can they do keep the water out of their homes and towns? Usually this meant building more dams and water retainers that may slow the water into *their* community but only pushes the water to other communities. The whole region of the US eastern seaboard is vulnerable, but communities focus on what they can do for themselves rather than confront their common problem.

Ovink's advice was to live with water rather than just resist it. But how to live with water? In Holland, Nijmegen and 38 other sites have developed the Room for the River program so that during flood periods parts of the area are prepared to be flooded. For example, an island is being created where apartment buildings will be built on the high ground and parks on the lower ground. These parks are made to be flooded to protect other parts of the island, but can be used when the rains stop and water retreats.

This plan requires a great deal of discussion among Dutch government units and citizens, who are accustomed to dykes and other buildings to keep water out but understandably worry about plans to "let water in" in order to live with it. Fortunately, the Dutch Water Boards have the authority and many years of experience leading joint efforts. They were able to help various partners discuss issues open-mindedly so that people through-out the region could understand the logic and purpose of the project.

Ovink wanted US coastal communities to experiment with innovative ways to live with water. To do that requires regional teamwork and a great deal of open-minded discussion among citizens and government leaders of these communities. Developing this large-scale teamwork has the potential to lead to long-term, powerful ways to cope with rising sea levels, a vital cooperative goal for all communities along the east coast.

Teambuilding Model for Effective Partnering

Alliances are designed to combine the diverse abilities of the partners. To take advantage of their alliance, partners must take each other's perspective so that they consider, know, and understand each other's ideas and strengths. Then they can integrate and apply their abilities and views to accomplish alliance goals.

Recent studies directly document the value of open-mindedness for alliance effectiveness and that cooperative goals are a strong foundation for this open-mindedness. (See the Research on the Teambuilding Model for Effective Partnering box.) These studies encourage Daniel, Joel, and others at Community Bank to apply their learning of the teambuilding model to their partnership with Mountain Bank. Community Bank can confidently propose to Mountain Bank that they use the teambuilding model to develop their partnership. Mountain Bank and Community Bank employees can together study the team model and its research to develop a common understanding of the nature of alliance they want and create concrete ways to improve their coordination and partnership.

Earlier chapters identify ideas and procedures that Community Bank and Mountain Bank can experiment with to develop cooperative relationships and open-minded discussion. For example, Chapter 4 suggests that employees from both banks form small problem-solving teams with each team given a group task; these tasks can range from completing analyses of the pork market in China to developing a conference to show farmers and feed and logistic companies how they can participate and benefit from the program. Executives from both banks can form a team to regularly assess the partnership's progress. These and other joint bank teams are small to encourage knee-to-knee and eye-to-eye communication and involvement. Members take time to get to know each other, perhaps have lunch or dinner together. They develop norms that guide how team members should work together. They reflect regularly on their working and develop concrete ways to strengthen their collaboration.

Joint Mountain–Community bank teams are important vehicles for strengthening cooperative goals and open-minded discussion so that the partnership results in cross-organizational teamwork. Productive teamwork is the means to develop and the desired outcome of partnering.

RESEARCH ON THE TEAMBUILDING MODEL FOR EFFECTIVE PARTNERING

Organizations, much as individuals and departments, are joining forces because they expect they can be more successful together than alone. Studies have directly documented that cooperative goals and open-minded discussion are powerful conditions for effective work across organizations as well as within teams.

The most active area of building teamwork across organizations is in the supply chain. Manufacturers, marketing, and logistic organizations are seeking to have long-term relationships so that they help each other add to the value chain. Evidence indicates that cooperative goals are important for helping supply chain partners attain quality delivery (Wong, Tjosvold, Wong, and Liu, 1999). Shared visions helped partners believe that they had cooperative goals that were important foundations for effective partnerships (Wu and Tjosvold, 2010).

Opportunistic behavior, where partners pursue their self-interests with guile, is thought to very much obstruct collaboration between organizations. Results from 103 pairs of customer and supplier organization partners indicate that, when they developed cooperative goals, they had little interest in opportunistic behavior (Wong, Tjosvold, and Yu, 2005). When partners believed that their goals were competitive or independent, they were more likely to pursue their self-interests opportunistically.

Although fierce competition between firms is considered a productive dynamic of the free market system, competitors are increasingly forming partnerships to work together to serve customers and solve problems (Jacobides, 2005; Rowley, Greve, Roa, Baum, and Shipilov, 2005). Although fears of opportunism would appear to be especially worrisome for competitors, competitor partners who developed cooperative relationships with each other, compared to competitive and independent ones, shared their ideas and resources, as they believed that they would both use this exchange for mutual benefit (Wong, Tjosvold, and Chen, 2010). Analyses from 95 outsourcing partnerships indicate that cooperative goals fostered open discussion and learning of effective practices that in turn resulted in business development.

The costs of coordinating, monitoring, and protecting one's organization from opportunism and other transaction costs can undermine the effectiveness of partnering. Results from 100 paired competitors supported the hypothesis that cooperative goals reduce transaction costs (Wong, Su, Tjosvold, and Chen, 2010). Specifically, competitive compared to cooperative goals increased transaction costs that resulted in ineffective collaboration. By strengthening cooperative goals and reducing competitive ones, competitors can manage their transaction costs and work together efficiently.

Competitors, especially as they are likely to have diverse ways of working, will confront frustrations and obstacles that must be negotiated if they are to collaborate effectively. Results have shown that those competitors that manage their conflicts cooperatively are able to strengthen their partnerships (Wong and Tjosvold, 2010). Having a strong relationship in terms of *guanxi* was found to be a foundation for this cooperative approach to managing conflict.

Teambuilding Model for Cross-culture Collaboration

Although based in the same industry and country, Community Bank and Mountain Bank have different values and ways of working. As the marketplace has become global, organizations are increasingly finding partners in countries with different and sometimes very different backgrounds and cultures. The teambuilding model can help partners appreciate and manage these cultural differences.

Organization cultures

Organizations have their own distinct origins, markets, and leadership styles that give rise to different cultures. Researchers have found that new employees need to be socialized into the company so that they know how to get things done; once socialized into the culture, they then become productive (Lu and Tjosvold, 2013). In an alliance, each partner is "new" to the other's culture.

Although they recognize that each bank has its own history and market position, Joel, Margaret, and their colleagues still surprise each other. Joel's team had assumed that their counterparts at Mountain Bank would always be in a "hurry-up" mode, pushing for things to be done now. Mountain Bank people had expected Community Bank people to complain that the partnership took time away from their home and leisure activities.

Partners have many little to big ways in which they are different from each other. Should meetings begin on the minute or is ten minutes past the scheduled time considered on time? Should they rely on emails or telephone calls? Should they expect crisis management weekly or semi-annually? How direct should they be in expressing their frustrations? To what extent should they openly articulate opposing views? How deferent should they be to each other and to their bosses?

Without agreeing on how they should work together, even little issues left unaddressed can disrupt. Mountain Bank may at first be willing to wait until Joel and colleagues finally get to their meeting and be able to forgive when they are late completing their tasks. If they also assume that they should not discuss their frustrations openly, they might conclude that they will have to just grin and bear the other's habits and ways of working. However, frustrations about meetings and deadlines as well as more substantial issues can build over time and result in deteriorated confidence, even covert and overt hostility to partners.

The teambuilding model reminds partners that they should discuss issues directly with each other and create ways of working with each other that are mutually beneficial. They realize that they should discuss when a partner's actions are undermining the feeling that they are working for mutual benefit and discussing issues open-mindedly.

Partners negotiate so that they develop a "third culture" of ways of working acceptable to both partners. They break out of the common belief that "as our way is better, we should do things our way" and the common impulse to push for their own ways. Instead, they develop ways of working that strengthen their partnership. They might adopt Community Bank's ways, or Mountain Bank's ways, or some combination of them or even something quite different. They make sure that this "third culture" helps them work together cooperatively and open-mindedly.

Cross-culture partnerships

East West Foods and soon Mountain Bank and Community Bank will work with the Chinese people who transport, market, and regulate pork imports. Working with Chinese people is different than working with Western people. As it is, misunderstandings occur within one team in one company in one culture; surely miscommunications between culturally diverse organizations are common. Diverse people often do not understand each other's messages in the ways that they were intended, leading to confusion and frustration.

Just looking at a Chinese dinner or reading the menu makes Westerners appreciate that Chinese people do things differently. These highly apparent differences help diverse people recognize that they might have to work carefully to communicate accurately.

Considerable research on cultural differences between East and West suggests that Chinese people, for example, tend to value the collective team whereas Westerners put more value on the individual. Compared to people in the West, they have also been found to accept and value power and status differences and believe that deference to authority is useful in many situations.

However, the evidence does not indicate that all Chinese persons have these values more than all Westerners. Cross-cultural researchers have proposed that diverse people should create the relationships that will help them work together, even if their societies tend to have different values (Bond, 2003). What is critical is for Joel and Margaret to understand how they can communicate and work effectively with the Chinese people they encounter, regardless of whether the values of the "average" person in China are different from the "average" person in the West.

Both experimental and field studies confirm that the teamwork model describes the conditions that help people from different cultures work together (Chen and Tjosvold, 2005, forthcoming; Chen, Tjosvold, and Su, 2005; Chen, Tjosvold, and Wu, 2008). Cooperative goals are a strong basis upon which culturally diverse people discuss their opposing views open-mindedly for mutual benefit. Although Margaret and Joel may not value the collective as much as their Chinese partners, findings indicate that to the extent that Chinese and Western people develop cooperative goals they will discuss their views open-mindedly and strengthen their partnership.

The teambuilding model can guide cross-cultural interaction and productive teamwork. Community Bank and Mountain Bank and their Chinese partners can use the teambuilding model to guide their development of a "fourth" culture. They need to create ways to collaborate that are known and suitable to all partners.

RESEARCH ON TEAMWORK WITH GOVERNMENT OFFICIALS

Around the world, governments matter and very much impact private business. Traditionally, the independence of private industry from government has been thought to be the most useful for developing business and an effective market economy more generally. However, research and practice have shown that developing a market-based, customer-oriented economy requires teamwork between government and industry (Lovett, Simmons, and Kali, 1999).

In a direct test of the teamwork model for relations between government and private industry, interviews of specific incidents were collected from 105 government officials and business people in Shanghai, China. Results supported the reasoning that cooperative, but not competitive or independent, goals strengthened their relationships, accomplished tasks, and fostered confidence that they will work productively in the future to develop their industry and the marketplace (Tjosvold, Peng, Chen, and Su, 2008). Results also indicate that open-minded discussions very much complemented cooperative goals to strengthen collaboration between managers and government officials.

China has taken a gradual approach, often called "step-by step," to economic reform, in particular to privatizing State Owned Enterprises (SOEs). When 200 government officials and SOE managers in Shanghai had cooperative, but not competitive and independent, goals, they applied their diverse perspectives and interests through open-minded discussions that in turn resulted in strengthened relationships, effective decisions that benefited employees, and developed the SOEs business (Tjosvold, Chen, Su, and Liao, 2009). In a survey of 119 pairs of government regulators and managers, results indicated that when they believed that their goals were cooperative, but not competitive, they fully exchanged their capabilities (Wong, Su, and Tjosvold, 2012). This integrative interaction in turn led businesses to conclude that the government regulators were competent, caring, and able to regulate industry effectively.

Cooperative relationships are also useful for helping government workers and citizens prepare for and manage natural disasters. Based on interviews of survivors from the 2008 Sichuan earthquake, findings indicate that cooperative goals between government and survivors facilitated *guanxi* with government officials and open-minded discussion that in turn promoted survivors' social support, satisfaction, reduced stress, and drew conclusions that government officials led effectively throughout the disaster (Chen and Tjosvold, 2011).

Moving to the Team Economy

Organizations are learning that forming partnerships can help them succeed in the marketplace. Companies have made their suppliers and marketing agents strategic partners who work together over time to improve quality to their customers and reduce costs. For example, automobile suppliers invest their resources to develop the innovative brakes its automobile client needs for future models.

Competitors are increasingly joining forces. In the 1980s, General Motors (GM) and Toyota developed a joint venture so that GM could learn Toyota manufacturing techniques and Toyota could improve its capabilities to access to the North American market. Since then, alliances between automobile companies have proliferated. The number of alliances continues to expand as competitors in many industries join together to take advantage of opportunities to serve customers effectively.

Government and corporate leaders are recognizing that they have common goals to develop high quality, safe products for customers, rewarding jobs for employees, and a safe and enhancing community for all. Rather than act as police and defendants, governments and business can work together as partners.

Organizations form partnerships for reasons similar to why individuals form teams: They can garner financial resources, specialists, and market access that one of them alone cannot. Organizations can be much more powerful together than alone.

Like members of a team, partners must coordinate to realize their potential. They must use their financial resources efficiently; specialists must integrate their knowledge so that the best solutions are implemented. The teambuilding model can be applied to strengthen partnerships as well as teams and organizations.

Business, social enterprises, and governments very much affect each other; crises and shortcomings in one of them present problems for the others. Financial crises, giant swings in stock markets, and worldwide worries about unemployment and underemployment are suggesting, to many government and business leaders, that their economies as well as their organizations must be more effectively managed.

We need more knowledge about how to manage our complex, highly interdependent economies. More direct research is needed to identify the extent and the ways that developing cooperative goals and open-minded discussion contribute to managing our economies and global market-places. Studies, however, have already shown that cooperative goals and open-minded discussion promote productive teamwork within a team, between departments, and across organizations and cultures.

Action Plans

Do less of:

- Assume that companies in the same market must compete.
- Assume partners have similar cultures because they are based in the same country.
- Require one partner to adopt the other's culture.
- Emphasize suspicion and opportunism.
- Assume diversity interferes with partnering.

Do more of:

- Explore partnering with competitors.
- Explore partnering with government agencies.
- Debate the value of the partnership open-mindedly.
- Develop team relationships across organizations and cultures.
- Integrate partners' complementary capabilities to serve customers.
- Assign important tasks to small joint partner teams.
- Forge ways of working that are acceptable to all partners.
- Appreciate the complexities and uncertainties of the team economy.
- Understand the opportunities of the team economy.

12

Reflection: Learning to be a Better Team

To err is human, to persist is diabolical.

Seneca

Daniel wanted to celebrate at a meeting of all employees. Government regulators had dropped the bank from their watch list. He was not surprised; the bank's loan quality and other measures were inching up. And, to be frank, the government's standards were modest. Still, it was direct confirmation that the bank was moving in the right direction and a good reason to celebrate. He thought that as everyone had contributed to the bank's progress, all should be informed and recognized.

He was in a reflective mood as well. There was much more that could be done, indeed, should be done. He was increasingly mindful of what he had learned at the Leadership Development Team (LTD) about the illusion of the status quo. There are always forces pushing on the current state of an organization, some pushing to strengthen and some to weaken it. The bank would either get stronger or weaker; it would not simply stay the same.

The bank must build upon constructive forces to get better or allow destructive forces to undermine it. Daniel was convinced that productive teamwork within the bank was fundamental to helping them strengthen constructive forces, cope with destructive ones, and take advantage of a changing marketplace.

He appreciated that he could draw upon his LTD readings and discussions as he thought of how to strengthen teamwork. He had assumed that leadership was mostly about action. What should he do to get people committed to their jobs and implement decisions? Now he realized that he had to understand both before and while he acted; he needed to have good ideas in order to analyze situations and decide what to do. Leadership is a performing art but it requires learning and understanding.

The teambuilding model of cooperative goals and open-minded discussion helped him analyze situations and take action. He and his colleagues had their own individual goals and interests but these could be aligned to form cooperative goals. Competitive and independent goals were alternatives that could at times be useful. But cooperative goals are the basis for open-minded discussions that coordinate actions and integrate ideas to solve problems, get things done, and strengthen relationships.

He knew that he had to live his understanding of teamwork. He had to develop cooperative goals with managers, indeed, with everyone in the organization and many outside it. He had to be prepared to express his own ideas but also to listen to and understand the views of others; he had to be willing to change his original thinking to incorporate the best ideas from others and then work to implement joint decisions. He saw that his team leadership had to begin with himself but then include everyone in the bank.

To lead he needed to "walk the talk" of teamwork. He also realized that the teambuilding model ideas helped him "talk and teach the talk". Employees could not be expected to "walk the talk" unless they knew what the talk was!

His employees and he want to do smart things. They are motivated to be a team when they understand how teamwork will pay off for them, their colleagues, and their customers. The teambuilding model's ideas are not merely nice sounding slogans but developed through considerable theorizing and evidence. Studies documented that cooperative goals and open-minded discussion pay off for teams, organizations, and people.

Employees had to believe that this teamwork was attainable as well as valuable. They wanted a clear understanding of how they could become a productive team with the confidence that they could achieve this. They wanted to know what they should do and what they should not do to strengthen their teamwork.

It's not just a few but all teammates who must understand and be committed in order to be a cooperative team. Individuals cannot work cooperatively alone. Their team members should also believe that their goals are cooperative and that they will discuss open-mindedly. Becoming a team is something team members do together. The teambuilding model clarifies their common destination and identifies paths to reach the kind of team that will serve them and their organization.

While Daniel's understanding of the teambuilding model suggested useful methods to build teamwork, it also helped him appreciate the challenges of maintaining it. Issues and conflicts will arise that might be avoided or handled antagonistically, leaving people feeling competitive and less willing to discuss issues open-mindedly. New employees may not understand or be committed to cooperative goals; they may be closed-minded and unskilled at discussion. He and the bank would have to keep working to strengthen their teamwork.

The more he thought about the employee celebration, the more he wanted discussion about important bank issues to complement the good news. He could not expect employees to be committed to the bank when they are unaware of what is happening at the bank. He realized that employees should ask questions and give opinions about the bank's directions. The meeting was an opportunity to involve employees in the bank as they discussed, posed questions, and expressed their own views.

The meeting should reinforce their cooperative goals and open-minded discussions. In discussion with Leslie, Daniel planned to form diverse teams with people from various departments; chairs would be arranged to be knee-to-knee and eye-to-eye; they would discuss their favorite movie to get to know each other better; they would have common tasks to discuss.

Daniel asked Joel and Raymond to give a briefing on recent developments with the joint venture with Mountain Bank. Groups would develop questions and raise concerns for Joel, Raymond, and Daniel to address.

Each group would keep notes of their questions and ideas. These notes would be collected and summarized, reinforcing that the bank valued employees' opinions and wanted them discussed seriously. These combined notes would give a snapshot of employee thinking.

Daniel would remind department teams to keep a folder with notes on their meetings. He would explain that the folder provided team members with an ongoing record of their progress in becoming a team. Managers would periodically review the folder for the teams they supervise, allowing them to be more proactive in leading and aiding their teams. Daniel would distribute a folder with forms that each department team would use to take norms and keep a record of their progress. Chapter 4 has examples of forms for taking notes.

Daniel also wanted to organize and lead a book club for people across the bank to discuss books on teamwork, leadership, and conflict management. Discussions would help people understand and apply ideas to their own work and team. Reading is good, Daniel would remind them, but reading and discussing together are better for understanding and applying.

As they developed more issues for employees to discuss, Daniel realized that the meeting was serious work. He would organize a party for the next Friday afternoon to celebrate and have fun together.

Daniel was realizing that he has power with his employees. He wanted employees to feel powerful too, as they have valuable resources and abilities. When staff members use their abilities to contribute to the bank, the more successful he is too. The more able and diverse employees are, the more they could accomplish together. He depends upon each employee; mistakes and unethical actions by any employee very much frustrate him as well as the bank.

The main message he wanted to send was that they were in this together. They could be much more successful working as a team than as individuals doing their own thing.

> "The president has come a long way, we have come a long way," Thomas said after the all employee meeting. "No more long-winded motivation lectures by our leaders."
>
> "We have more paperwork though," Joel said. "We're to keep a team folder of notes of our meetings."
>
> "It's a way for us to reflect on our team and plan how we can learn and improve step-by-step," Courtney said.

The team felt good about the employee meeting. They met and worked with people from other departments. They felt better prepared to initiate discussions with other departments and to deal with crises as they arose.

They enjoyed updating the other teams on the pork for export to China partnership. They were impressed about how the operations group had taken the initiative to develop a community garden on vacant land owned by the bank. The project was a good thing to do, and a good marketing tool as well.

They liked the client service group's suggestion to join local groups in supporting eye-care in Africa. These groups organize 20 ophthalmologists in temporary clinics in West Africa and other less developed nations. In a couple of weeks, the group can treat and give proper eye classes to help thousands see for years to come. The bank's community is much larger than the city's southwest neighborhood.

"Operations and client services are helping us," Thomas said. "We should let them know that we appreciate what they're doing for the community and what they are doing for the bank's community standing."

"People can do many good things when they're organized," Courtney said.

The team then discussed business issues about the Donaldson loan, the pork for export venture, and other projects. They then turned to preparing for the celebration on Friday.

"How are we going to let the rest of the bank know more about the personality and character of our team?" Thomas asked. "Some teams are planning skits."

"I'll be happy if we can develop a skit that really communicates who we are," Joel said.

"We began thinking about teamwork in terms of a team bonus," Thomas said. "If we were paid, then we would work together."

"Team bonus is good," Courtney said. "The better one member does, the better others do in terms of hard cold cash."

"Agree, but working together takes much more than having a team bonus," Joel said. "I had to learn to relax about being dependent on others, understanding each other's goals, appreciating each other's ability, learning how to help each other, and feeling grateful for being helped. It's a long list."

"We also had to change our ideas about leadership," Thomas said. "We need leadership to work together but we don't need to be bossed."

"Daniel has shown us a viable alternative to micro-managing," Courtney said.

"He helps us develop good relationships, even with those outside the company," Thomas said. "Then we can get things done."

"He's powerful but so are we," Courtney said.

"We're each powerful," Joel said. "It's often said that there's no 'I' in team, as if we suppress who we are to be on the team. Not true."

"We're a team but we're all individuals too," Thomas said.

"Let's use our skit to tell others that we have three 'I's in this team," Joel said.

Breaking Out of "Either-Or" Thinking

Popular, but misleading "either-or" thinking frustrates efforts to build a team organization. Ideas of the individual versus the team and cooperation versus conflict reinforce each other and create the illusion of being a systematic, practical way of thinking. Talked about so long and discussed so often, these ideas are considered so common sense that no debate is needed. However, people at Community Bank had to break out of these habits to put teamwork ideas into place.

The individual and the group

The choice is often posed as one between the individual or the group. An organization can foster groups or individuals; a society is either collectivist or individualistic; a person can be independent or a team player. But these are false choices.

Psychological and organizational research does not support this "either the individual or the group" reasoning. Individuals are not fulfilled isolated from others; just having yourself on your side is not enough to develop yourself. People need the support of others and their feedback to know and value themselves. For individuals to strengthen and use their specialized expertise, they need groups and organizations.

Groups and organizations need creative, independent thinkers, not passive conformers. A central rationale for a team is to combine the perspectives, energies, and specialties of a diverse people. The Chicago businessman, William Wrigley, put it this way: "If two people in business always agree, one of them is unnecessary."

Organizations and societies can promote both teams and individuals or undermine teams and individuals. An individual can work for him or herself and for the team at the same time. Cooperative teams provide rich, supportive, challenging environments that stimulate individuality and independent thought. Teams require the integration of diverse perspectives and coordination of effort to succeed. Individuals make a difference by having an impact on and through their cooperative teams. People and the organization both win when their individuality and cooperative teamwork are developed.

Conflict and cooperation

A related misleading choice is between cooperation or conflict, between productive harmony or destructive discord. Community Bank employees are learning that they should choose both cooperation and conflict.

Conflict breathes life into cooperation. Through open-minded controversy, teammates integrate their views and solve problems. Conflict is a medium for them to find fair ways of dividing their work and sharing the benefits of their cooperative effort that strengthen their commitment to work cooperatively. To choose cooperation is to choose conflict.

Through cooperation and conflict, people express their individuality and have their worth affirmed. They identify their interests so that others respond to them. They clarify their thinking and have it incorporated into the team's decision. They are confronted to upgrade their abilities and apply them for the benefit of their team and themselves.

There are, of course, real tradeoffs in many decisions: If one group gets its full budget, other groups do not. That compromises must be made and scarcity of resources managed does not mean, though, that basic goals and aspirations are competitive. Teammates have to negotiate their agendas and interests so that they can help each other accomplish their goals.

Managers and employees need to break out of tradeoff thinking that they can support the team or the individual, develop cooperation or conflict. Individuals and teams are not opposites but complement each other. Leaders and teams need not struggle for control; the power of one reinforces the power of the other. Community Bank employees were learning that their differences and conflicts did not mean disunity but were opportunities to reaffirm and strengthen their cooperative unity.

Applying Teambuilding Ideas to Build a Learning Organization

Daniel, Joel, and others at Community Bank had come to appreciate Kurt Lewin's adage of that "There is *nothing so practical as a good theory.*" Through discussion, Joel and others had come to a shared conviction that they wanted the team-building model of cooperative goals and open-minded discussion ideas to be their common ideals. These ideas could serve as guides for how to work with people throughout the bank. They were using the teamwork model to build a learning organization able to identify challenges and opportunities and adapt by creating new solutions for their bank (Argyris and Schon, 1978).

The model of cooperative goals and open-minded discussion can also guide how Community Bank, Mountain Bank, and East West Foods work together. The model provides an explicit framework they can use to forge a united venture out of several organizations.

The teamwork model, however, is not a script to follow. Community Bank employees have to deepen their understanding of cooperation and open-mindedness, develop and implement their own plans for how to apply them, and then reflect and modify. They are learning that understanding, action, and reflection reinforce each other.

The loan officers are learning to build cooperative relationships with people throughout the organization. Through these relationships, they can engage in effective dialogue and integrate their ideas and efforts. Intellectual, rational discussions are built on personal bonds of trust and reliance. Impersonal, fragmented relationships create the suspicion that undermines communication and conflict management. Joel's group wants to know their colleagues and to be known to them.

Working as a team is built into human beings. We have been surviving and thriving through teamwork for millennia. However, we are facing new conditions and new pitfalls.

Abraham Lincoln has given us good advice: "Still the question recurs 'Can we do better?' The dogmas of the quiet past are inadequate to the stormy present. The occasion is piled high with difficulty, and we must rise with the occasion. As our case is new, so we must think anew, and act anew."

Productive teamwork is vital to help us meet emerging global challenges from producing quality food for a growing population to providing security from violence. To succeed, we must develop teamwork in new types of organizations between people who have little experience collaborating with each other. Manufacturers need to work with environmentalists, business people with government officials, communities with each other, and developed with developing nations to reform the ways we make and distribute goods and services in order to cope with climate changes. Knowledge of productive teamwork can help us refine ways to work together so that we cope and flourish.

Action Plans

Do less of:

- Reflect on relationships by yourself.
- Take credit for company achievements.
- Ask others to cooperate, but not yourself.
- Equate cooperation with the absence of conflict.
- Assume we cannot work together because the world has changed so rapidly.

Do more of:

- Teach and walk the talk of teamwork.
- Recognize that teams and organizations are getting stronger or weaker.
- Use company-wide meetings to keep everyone informed and help people get to know each other.
- Reflect regularly and keep records on how team members are working together.
- Brainstorm periodically how to strengthen teamwork.
- Appreciate that there are many "I"s in team.
- Realize that people have thrived for millennia by working together but now must do so under rapidly changing conditions.

References

1 Teambuilding is Necessary

Bolger, N. and Eckenrode, J., 1991. Social relationships, personality, and anxiety during a major stress event. *Journal of Personality and Social Psychology*, 61(3), pp. 440–9.

Brockner, J., 1988. *Self-esteem: Theory, Research, the Practice*. Lexington, MA: Lexington Books.

Eisenberger, R., Fasolo, P., and Davis-LaMastro, V., 1990. Perceived organizational support and employee diligence, commitment, and innovation. *Journal of Applied Psychology*, 75, pp. 51–9.

Jecker, J. and Landy, D., 1969. Liking a person as a function of doing him a favor. *Human Relations*, 22(4), pp. 371–8.

Kirmeyer, S. and Lin, T., 1987. Social support: Its relationship to observed communication with peers and superiors. *Academy of Management Journal*, 30(1), pp. 138–51.

McClelland, D.C., 1987. *Human Motivation*. New York: Cambridge University Press.

Mead, G.H., 1934. *Mind, Self and Society*. Chicago: University of Chicago Press.

Nayar, V., 2010. *Employees First, Customers Second*. Boston, MA: Harvard Business School Publishing.

Seligman, M., 1988. Boomer blues. *Psychology Today*, 22, pp. 50–5.

Shenk, J.W., 2009. What makes us happy? *The Atlantic*, [online] Available at: ‹http://www.theatlantic.com/magazine/archive/2009/06/what-makes-us-happy/307439/2/?single_page=true› [Accessed 1 June 2009].

Tjosvold, D., Meredith, L. and Wong, C., 1998. Coordination to market technology: The contribution of cooperative goals and interaction. *Journal of High Technology Management Research*, 9(1), pp. 1–15.

2   What Makes Teams Effective?

Deutsch, M., 1949. A theory of cooperation and competition. *Human Relations*, 2, pp. 129–52.

Deutsch, M., 1973. *The Resolution of Conflict*. New Haven, CT: Yale University Press.

Hogan, R., Curphy, G. J. and Hogan, J., 1994. What we know about leadership: Effectiveness and personality. *American Psychologist*, 49(6), pp. 493–504.

Johnson, D.W., 1970. *Social Psychology of Education*. New York: Holt, Rhinehart and Winston.

Johnson, D.W., 2003. Social interdependence: interrelationships among theory, research and practice. *American Psychologist*, 58(11), pp. 934–45.

Johnson, D.W. and Johnson, R.T., 1974. Instructional structure: Cooperative, competitive, or individualization. *Review of Educational Research*, 44(2), pp. 213–40.

Johnson, D.W. and Johnson, R.T., 1989. *Leading the Cooperative School*. Edina, MN: Interaction Book Company.

Johnson, D.W. and Johnson, R.T., 2005. New developments in social interdependence theory. *Genetic, Social, and General Psychology Monographs*, 131(4), pp. 285–358.

Johnson, D.W., Johnson, R.T., and Tjosvold, D., 2014. Constructive controversy: The value of intellectual opposition. In: M. Deutsch, P.T. Coleman and E. Marcus, eds. *The Handbook of Conflict Resolution: Theory and Practice*. San Francisco: Jossey-Bass. pp. 69–91.

Kanter, R.M., 1991. Championing change; an interview with Bell Atlantic's CEO Raymond Smith. *Harvard Business Review*, 69(1), pp. 118–30.

Karau, S.J., Williams, K.D. (1993). Social loafing: A meta-analytic review and theoretical integration. *Journal of Personality and Social Psychology*, 65, 681–706.

Kouzes, J.M. and Posner, B.Z., 2008. *The Leadership Challenge*. San Francisco, CA: Jossey-Bass.

Latané, B., Williams, K., and Harkins, S. (1979). Many hands make light the work: The causes and consequences of social loafing. *Journal of Personality and Social Psychology*, 37, 822–32.

Schmidt, F., 2010. Detecting and correcting the lies that data tell. *Perspectives on Psychological Science*, 5, pp. 233–42.

3   Applying the Model: The Method Reinforces the Message

Chen, N.Y., Tjosvold, D., Huang, X. and Xu, D., 2011. Newcomer socialization in China: Effects of team values and goal interdependence. *The International Journal of Human Resource Management*, 22(16), pp. 3317–37.

Chen, N.Y.F., Lu, J.F., Tjosvold, D., and Lin, C., 2008. Effects of team goal inter-dependence on newcomer socialization: An experiment in China. *Journal of Applied Social Psychology*, 38(1), pp. 198–214.

Halpern, D.F. and Hakel, M.D. eds., 2002. *Applying the Science of Learning to the University and Beyond. New Directions for Teaching and Learning*. San Francisco: Jossey-Bass.

Johnson, D.W., Druckman, D., and Dansereau, D., 1994. Training in teams. In: D. Druckman and R. Bjork, eds. *Learning, Remembering, Believing: Enhancing Human Performance*. Washington, DC: National Academy Press. pp. 140–70.

Keefe, P.R., 2013. Rocket Man: How an unemployed blogger confirmed that Syria had used chemical weapons. *The New Yorker*, November 25.

Lu, J.F., Tjosvold, D., and Shi, K., 2010. Team training in China: Testing and apply-ing the theory of cooperation and competition. *Journal of Applied Social Psychology*, 40(1), pp. 101–34.

Lu, S.C. and Tjosvold, D., 2013. Socialization tactics: Antecedents for goal inter-dependence and newcomer adjustment and retention. *Journal of Vocational Behavior*, 83(3), 245–54.

Tjosvold, D., Chen, N.Y.F., Huang, X., and Xu, D., 2014. Developing cooperative teams to support individual performance and well being in a call center in China. *Group Decision Making and Negotiation*, 23(2), pp. 325–48.

Tjosvold, D., Tang, M.L., and West, M.A., 2004. Reflexivity for team innovation in China: The contribution of goal interdependence. *Group and Organization Management*, 29(5), pp. 540–60.

Tjosvold, D., Yu, Z.Y., and Hui, C., 2004. Team learning from mistakes: The con-tribution of cooperative goals and problem-solving. *Journal of Management Studies*, 41(7), pp. 1223–45.

4 Getting Started

Gawande, A., 2013. Slow Ideas: Some innovations spread fast. How do you speed the ones that don't? *The New Yorker*, July 29.

Johnson, D.W., Maruyama, G., Johnson, R., Nelson, D., and Skon, L., 1981. Effects of cooperative, competitive, and individualistic goal structure on achievement: A meta-analysis. *Psychological Bulletin*, 89: 47–62.

Johnson, D.W. and Johnson, R., 2005. New developments in social interdepend-ence theory. *Psychology Monographs*, 131, 285–358.

McClelland, D.C., 1987. *Human Motivation*. New York: Cambridge University Press.

Tjosvold, D., Chen, N.Y., Huang, X. and Xu, D., 2012. Developing cooperative teams to support individual performance and well being in a call center in China. *Group Decision Making and Negotiation*. Advance online publication. doi: 10.1007/s10726-012-9314-6.

5   Leadership for Teamwork, Teamwork for Leadership

Abu Bakar, H., Dilbeck, K.E., and McCroskey, J.C., 2010, Mediating role of supervisory communication practices on relations between leader-member exchange and perceived employee commitment to workgroup. *Communication Monographs*, 77(4), pp. 637–56.

Avolio, B.J., Walumbwa, F.O., and Weber, T., 2009. Leadership: Current theories, research and future directions. *Annual Review of Psychology*, 60, pp. 421–49.

Bhatnagar, D. and Tjosvold, D., 2012. Leader values for constructive controversy and team effectiveness in India. *The International Journal of Human Resource Management*, 23(1), pp. 109–25.

Chen, G., Liu, C.H., and Tjosvold, D., 2005. Conflict management for effective top management teams and innovation in China. *Journal of Management Studies*, 42(2), pp. 277–300.

Chen, N.Y.F. and Tjosvold, D., 2007. *Guanxi* and leader member relationships between American managers and Chinese employees: Open-minded dialogue as mediator. *Asia Pacific Journal of Management*, 24(2), pp. 171–89.

Chen, G. and Tjosvold, D., 2012. Shared rewards and goal interdependence for psychological safety among departments in China. *Asia Pacific Journal of Management*, 29(2), pp. 433–52.

Dulebohn, J.H., Bommer, W.H., Liden, R.C., Brouer, R.L., and Ferris, G.R., 2012. A meta-analysis of antecedents and consequences of leader-member exchange integrating the past with an eye toward the future. *Journal of Management*, 38(6), pp. 1715–59.

Graen, G.B. and Uhl-Bien, M., 1995. Relationship-based approach to leadership: Development of leader-member exchange (LMX) theory of leadership over 25 years: Applying a multi-level multi-domain perspective. *The Leadership Quarterly*, 6(2), pp. 219–47.

Hogan, R., Curphy, G.J., and Hogan, J., 1994. What we know about leadership: Effectiveness and personality. *American psychologist*, 49(6), pp. 493–504.

Johnson, D.W. and Johnson, R.T., 2005. New developments in social interdependence theory. *Genetic, Social, and General Psychology Monographs*, 131(4), pp. 285–358.

Karriker, J.H. and Williams, M.L., 2009. Organizational justice and organizational citizenship behavior: A mediated multifoci model? *Journal of Management*, 35(1), pp. 112–35.

Kath, L.M., Marks, K.M., and Ranney, J., 2010. Safety climate dimensions, leader–member exchange, and organizational support as predictors of upward safety communication in a sample of rail industry workers. *Safety Science*, 48(5), pp. 643–50.

Kouzes, J.M. and Posner, B.Z., 2005. Leading in cynical times. *Journal of Management Inquiry*, 14(4), pp. 357–64.

Law, K.S., Wang, H., and Hui, C., 2010. Currencies of exchange and global LMX: How they affect employee task performance and extra-role performance. *Asia Pacific Journal of Management*, 27(4), pp. 625–46.

Lee, J. and Jablin, F.M., 1995. Maintenance communication in superior-subordinate work relationships. *Human Communication Research*, 22(2), pp. 220–57.

Liden, R.C. and Graen, G.B., 1980. Generalizability of the vertical dyad linkage model of leadership. *Academy of Management Journal*, 23(3), pp. 451–65.

Ozer, M., 2008. Personal and task-related moderators of leader-member exchange among software developers. *Journal of Applied Psychology*, 93(5), pp. 1174–82.

Tjosvold, D., Hui, C., and Law, K.S., 1998. Empowerment in the manager-employee relationship in Hong Kong: Interdependence and controversy. *Journal of Social Psychology*, 138(5), pp. 624–37.

Tjosvold, D., Poon, M., and Yu, Z.Y., 2005. Team effectiveness in China: Cooperative conflict for relationship building. *Human Relations*, 58(3), pp. 341–67.

Wong, A.S.H, Liu, Y., and Tjosvold, D. 2014. *Servant Leadership for Team Conflict Management, Coordination, and Customer Relationships*. Presented at the 2014 Academy of Management Annual Meeting, Philadelphia.

Wong, A.S.H. and Tjosvold, D., 2010. Guanxi and conflict management for effective partnering with competitors in China. *British Journal of Management*, 21(3), pp. 772–88.

Wong, A.S.H., Wei, L., and Tjosvold, D., 2014. Business and regulators partnerships: Government transformational leadership for constructive conflict management. *Asia Pacific Journal of Management*, 31(2), pp. 497–522.

Xu, E., Huang, X., Lam, C.K., and Miao, Q., 2012. Abusive supervision and work behaviors: The mediating role of LMX. *Journal of Organizational Behavior*, 33(4), pp. 531–43.

Xu, J. and Thomas, H.C., 2011. How can leaders achieve high employee engagement? *Leadership & Organization Development Journal*, 32(4), pp. 399–416.

Zhang, X.A., Cao, Q., and Tjosvold, D., 2011. Linking transformational leadership and team performance: A conflict management approach. *Journal of Management Studies*, 48(7), pp. 1586–611.

7   Working Open-Mindedly

Alper, S., Tjosvold, D. and Law, K.S., 1998. Interdependence and controversy in group decision making: Antecedents to effective self-managing teams. *Organizational Behavior and Human Decision Processes*, 74(1), pp. 33–52.

Alper, S., Tjosvold, D., and Law, K.S., 2000. Conflict management, efficacy, and performance in organizational teams. *Personnel Psychology*, 53(3), 625–42. doi: 10.1111/j.1744-6570.2000.tb00216.x.

Beersman, B., Hollenbeck, J.R., Humphrey, S., Moon, H., and Ilgen, D.R., 2003. Cooperation, competition, and team performance: Toward a contingency approach. *Academy of Management Journal*, 46(5), pp. 572–90.

Edmondson, A.C., 2012. Teamwork on the fly: How to master the new art of teaming. *Harvard Business Review*, April, pp. 72–80.

Johnson, D.W., 1967. The use of role reversal in intergroup competition. *Journal of Personality and Social Psychology*, 7, pp. 135–41.

Johnson, D.W., 1971a. Effectiveness of role reversal: Actor or listener. *Psychological Reports*, 28, pp. 275–82.

Johnson, D.W., 1971b. Effects of warmth of interaction, accuracy of understanding, and the proposal of compromises on listener's behavior. *Journal of Counseling Psychology*, 18(3), pp. 207–16.

Johnson, D.W., Johnson, R.T., and Tjosvold, D., 2006. Constructive controversy: The value of intellectual opposition. In: M. Deutsch, P.T. Coleman, and E. Marcus, eds. *The Handbook of Conflict Resolution: Theory and Practice*. San Francisco: Jossey-Bass. pp. 69–91.

Laughlin, P.R., 2011. *Group Problem Solving*. Princeton, New Jersey: Princeton University Press.

Richter, F. and Tjosvold, D., 1980. Effects of student participation in classroom decision-making on attitudes, peer interaction, motivation, and learning. *Journal of Applied Psychology*, 65(1), pp. 74–80.

Tjosvold, D., 1984. Effects of crisis orientation on managers' approach to controversy in decision making. *Academy of Management Journal*, 27(1), pp. 130–8.

Tjosvold, D., 1985. Implications of controversy research for management. *Journal of Management*, 11(3), pp. 19–35.

Tjosvold, D., 1987. Participation: A close look at its dynamics. *Journal of Management*, 13(4), pp. 141–52.

Tjosvold, D., 1990. Flight crew coordination to manage safety risks. *Group and Organization Studies*, 15(2), pp. 177–91.

Tjosvold, D. and Deemer, D.K., 1980. Effects of controversy within a cooperative or competitive context on organizational decision-making. *Journal of Applied Psychology*, 65(5), pp. 590–5.

Tjosvold, D. and Field, R.H.G., 1983. Effects of social context on consensus and majority vote decision making. *Academy of Management Journal*, 26(3), pp. 500–6.

Tjosvold, D. and Johnson, D.W., 1977. The effects of controversy on cognitive perspective taking. *Journal of Educational Psychology*, 69(6), pp. 679–85.

Tjosvold, D. and Johnson, D.W., 1978. Controversy within a cooperation or competitive context and cognitive perspective-taking. *Contemporary Educational Psychology*, 3(4), pp. 376–86.

Tjosvold, D., Peng, A.C., Chen, N.Y. and Su, S.F., 2013. Individual decision-making in organizations: contribution of uncertainty and controversy in China. *Group Decision and Negotiation*, 22(4), pp. 801–21.

Tjosvold, D., Wong, A.S.H., and Chen, N.Y.F. 2014. Constructively managing conflicts in organizations. *Annual Review of Organizational Psychology and Organizational Behavior*, 1, pp. 545–68.

8 Managing Conflict Constructively

Dana, D., 2005. *Managing Differences: How to Build Better Relationships at Work and Home*. 4th edn. Prairie Mission, KS: MTI Publications.

Deutsch, M., 1973. *The Resolution of Conflict*. New Haven, CT: Yale University Press.

Johnson, D.W., Johnson, R.T., and Tjosvold, D., 2014. Constructive controversy: The value of intellectual opposition. In: M. Deutsch, P.T. Coleman, and E. Marcus, eds. *The Handbook of Conflict Resolution: Theory and Practice*. San Francisco: Jossey-Bass. pp. 69–91.

Tjosvold, D., 1991. *The Conflict-Positive Organization: Stimulate Diversity and Create Unity*. Reading, MA: Addison-Wesley.

Tjosvold, D., 2007. The conflict-positive organization: It depends upon us. *Journal of Organizational Behavior*, 29, pp. 19–28.

Tjosvold, D., 2002. Managing anger for teamwork in Hong Kong: Goal interdependence and open-mindedness. *Asian Journal Social Psychology*, 5, pp. 107–23.

Tjosvold, D., Huang, Y.U., Johnson, D.W., and Johnson, R.T., 2008. Is the way you resolve conflicts related to your psychological health? An empirical investigation. *Peace and Conflict: Journal of Peace Psychology*, 14(4), pp. 1–34.

Tjosvold, D. and Morishima, M., 1999. Grievance resolution: Perceived goal interdependence and interaction patterns. *Industrial Relations*, 54(3), pp. 529–50.

Tjosvold, D., Morishima, M., and Belsheim, J.A., 1999. Complaint handling on the shop floor: Cooperative relationships and open-minded strategies. *International Journal of Conflict Management*, 10(1), pp. 45–68.

Tjosvold, D. and Su, F.S., 2007. Managing anger and annoyance in organizations in China: The role of constructive controversy. *Group and Organization Management*, 32(3), pp. 260–89.

Tjosvold, D. and Sun, H. 2002. Understanding conflict avoidance: Relationship, motivations, actions, and consequences. *International Journal of Conflict Management*, 13(2), pp. 142–64.

Tjosvold, D., Wong, A., and Chen, NY.F., 2014. Cooperative and competitive conflict management in organizations. In: O.B. Ayoko, N.M. Ashkanasy, and K.A. Jehn, eds. *Handbook of Conflict Management Research*. Cheltenham, UK: Edward Elgar Publishing. pp. 33–50.

9 Teamwork with Customers

Avery, J., Fournier, S., and Wittenbraker, J., 2014. Unlock the mysteries of your customer relationships. *Harvard Business Review*, 92(7), pp. 72–81.

Kouzes, J.M. and Posner, B.Z., 1995. *The Leadership Challenge: How to Keep Getting Extraordinary Things Done in Organizations*. San Francisco: Jossey-Bass.

Merlo, O., Eisingerich, A.B., and Auh, S., 2014. Why customer participation matters. *MIT Sloan Management Review*, 55(2), pp. 81–8.

Rust, R.T., Moorman, C., and Bhalla, G., 2010. Rethinking marketing. *Harvard Business Review*, 88(1/2), pp. 94–101.

Tjosvold, D., 1993. *Teamwork for Customers: Building Organizations that Take Pride in Serving*. San Francisco: Jossey-Bass.

Tjosvold, D. and Wong, C.L., 1994. Working with customers: Cooperation and competition in relational marketing. *Journal of Marketing Management*, 10(4), pp. 297–310.

Wong, C.L. and Tjosvold, D., 1995. Goal interdependence and quality in services marketing. *Psychology & Marketing*, 12, pp. 189–205.

Zemke, R. and Schaaf, D., 1989. *The Service Edge: 101 Companies that Profit from Customer Care*. New York: New American Library.

10 Team Organization: Departments Working Together

Beersman, B., Hollenbeck, J.R., Humphrey, S.E., Moon, H., Colon, D.E., and Ilgen, D.R., 2003. Cooperation, competition, and team performance: toward a contingency approach. *Academy of Management Journal*, 46(5), pp. 572–90.

Bethune, G. (1999). *From Worse to First: Behind the Scene of Continental's Remarkable Comeback*. New York: John Wiley & Sons.

Carmeli, A., Gilat, G., and Waldman, D.A., 2007. The role of perceived organizational performance in organizational identification, adjustment and job performance. *Journal of Management Studies*, 44(6), pp. 972–92.

Chen, G., Liu, C.H., and Tjosvold, D., 2005. Conflict management for effective top management teams and innovation in China. *Journal of Management Studies*, 42(2), pp. 277–300.

Chen, G. and Tjosvold, D., 2008. Organizational values and procedures as antecedents for goal interdependence and collaborative effectiveness. *Asia Pacific Journal of Management*, 25(1), pp. 93–112.

Chen, G. and Tjosvold, D., 2012. Shared rewards and goal interdependence for psychological safety among departments in China. *Asia Pacific Journal of Management*, 29(2), pp. 433–52.

Chen, G., Tjosvold, D., and Liu, C.H., 2006. Cooperative goals and leader people and productivity values: Their contribution to top management teams in China. *Journal of Management Studies*, 43(5), pp. 1177–200.

Haslam, S.A., Jettern, J., Postmes, T., and Haslam, C., 2009. Social identity, health and well-being: An emerging agenda for applied psychology. *Applied Psychology: An International Review*, 58(1), pp. 1–23.

Henderson, R., 1994. Managing innovation in the information age. *Harvard Business Review*, January–February, pp. 100–5.

Johnson, D.W. and Johnson, R.T., 2005. New developments in social interdependence theory. *Genetic, Social, and General Psychology Monographs*, 131(4), pp. 285–358.

Lagace, M., 2003. *Guiding Growth: How Vision Keeps Companies on Course*. [online] Available at: ‹http://hbswk.hbs.edu/archive/3342.html› [Accessed February 24, 2003].

Lee, C., Farh, J.L., and Chen, Z.J., 2011. Promoting group potency in project teams: The importance of group identification. *Journal of Organizational Behavior*, 32(8), pp. 1147–62.

Nichols, N.A., 1994. Scientific management at Merck: An interview with CFO Judy Lewent. *Harvard Business Review*, January–February, pp. 89–99.

Poon, M., Pike, R., and Tjosvold, D., 2001. Budget participation, goal interdependence and controversy: A study of a Chinese public utility. *Management Accounting Research*, 12(1), pp. 101–18.

Rhoades, L. and Eisenberger, R., 2002. Perceived organizational support: A review of the literature. *Journal of Applied Psychology*, 87(4), pp. 698–714.

Tjosvold, D., Johnson, D.W., Johnson, R.T., and Sun, H., 2003. Can interpersonal competition be constructive within organizations? *Journal of Psychology*, 137(1), pp. 63–84.

Tjosvold, D., Johnson, D.W., and Sun, H., 2006. Competitive motives and strategies: Understanding constructive competition. *Group Dynamics: Theory, Research, & Practice*, 10(2), pp. 87–99.

Tjosvold, D. and MacPherson, R.C., 1996. Joint hospital management by physicians and nursing administrators. *Health Care Management Review*, 21(3), pp. 43–54.

Tjosvold, D. and Poon, M., 1998a. Using and valuing accounting information: Joint decision making between accountants and retail managers. *Group Decision and Negotiation*, 7(4), pp. 1–19.

Tjosvold, D. and Poon, M., 1998b. Dealing with scarce resources: Openminded interaction for resolving budget conflicts. *Group & Organization Management*, 23(3), pp. 237–55.

Waber, B. (2013). *People Analytics: How Social Sensing Technology Will Transform Business and What it Tells Us About the Future of Work*. New Jersey: FT Press.

11 Partnering with Competitors and Government: Moving to the Team Economy

Bond, M.H., 2003. Cross-cultural social psychology and the real world of culturally diverse teams and dyads. In: D. Tjosvold and K. Leung, eds, *Cross-Cultural Foundations: Traditions for Managing in a Cross-Cultural World*. Farnham, UK: Ashgate, pp. 43–58.

Chen, Y.F. and Tjosvold, D., 2005. Cross cultural leadership: Goal interdependence and leader-member relations in foreign ventures in China. *Journal of International Management*, 11(3), pp. 417–39.

Chen, Y.F. Tjosvold, D., and Su, S.F., 2005. Goal interdependence for working across cultural boundaries: Chinese employees with foreign managers. *International Journal of Intercultural Relations*, 29(4), pp. 429–47.

Chen, Y.F., Tjosvold, D., and Wu, P.G., 2008. Foreign managers' *guanxi* with Chinese employees: Effects of warm-heartedness and reward distribution on negotiation. *Group Decision and Negotiation*, 17, pp. 79–96.

Chen, N.Y.F. and Tjosvold, D., 2011. *Disaster Recovery from the 2008 Great Sichuan Earthquake in China: Constructive Controversy and Relationships*. Presented at the 2011 Academy of Management Annual Meeting, San Antonio, TX.

Chen, Y.F. and Tjosvold, D., forthcoming. Relationships between Western managers and Chinese employees for trust and commitment. *Asia Pacific Journal of Human Resources*.

Gomory, R., 2010. A time for action: Jobs, prosperity and national goals. *Huffington Post*. [online] Available at:‹http://www.huffingtonpost.com/ralph-gomory/a-time-for-action-jobs- pr_b_434698.html› [Accessed March 27, 2010].

Jacobides, M.G., 2005. Industry change through vertical disintegration: How and why markets emerged in mortgage banking. *Academy of Management Journal*, 48(3), pp. 465–98.

Lovett, S., Simmons, L.C., and Kali, R., 1999. *Guanxi* versus the market: ethics and efficiency. *Journal of International Business Studies*, 30(2), pp. 231–48.

Lu, S.C. and Tjosvold, D., 2013. Socialization tactics: Antecedents for goal interdependence and newcomer adjustment and retention. *Journal of Vocational Behavior*, 83(3), pp. 245–54.

Rowley, T., Greve, H.R., Roa, H., Baum, J.A.C., and Shipilov, A.V., 2005. Time to break up: Social and instrumental antecedents of firm exits from exchange cliques. *Academy of Management Journal*, 48(3), pp. 499–520.

Shorto, R., 2014. How to Think Like the Dutch in a Post-Sandy World. *New York Times Magazine*. [online] Available at:<http://www.nytimes.com/2014/04/13/magazine/how-to-think-like-the-dutch-in-a-post-sandy-world.html?_r=0> [Accessed April 9, 2014].

Tjosvold, D., Peng, A.C., Chen, Y.F., and Su, F., 2008. Business and government interdependence in China: Cooperative goals to develop business and industry. *Asia Pacific Journal of Management*, 25(2), pp. 225–49.

Tjosvold, D., Chen,Y.F., Su, F., and Liao, Y., 2009. *Relationships and Discussion for Privatizing State Owned Enterprises in China: Deciding Next Steps.* Presented at the 2009 Academy of Management Annual Meeting, Chicago, Illinois, USA.

Wong, A., Su, S.F., and Tjosvold, D., 2012. Developing business trust in government through resource exchange in China. *Asia Pacific Journal of Management*, 29(4), pp. 2027–43.

Wong, A., Su, F.S., Tjosvold, D., and Chen, Y.F., 2010. *Goal Interdependence to Manage Transaction Costs in Partnering with Competitors.* Presented at the 2010 Biennial Conference of the International Association for Chinese Management Research (IACMR), Shanghai, China.

Wong, A.S.H. and Tjosvold, D., 2010. *Guanxi* and conflict management for effective partnering with competitors in China. *British Journal of Management*, 21(3), pp. 772–88.

Wong, A.S.H., Tjosvold, D., and Chen, N.Y.F., 2010. Managing outsourcing to develop business: Goal interdependence for sharing effective business practices in China. *Human Relations*, 63, pp. 1563–86.

Wong, A., Tjosvold, D., Wong, W., and Liu, C.K., 1999. Cooperative and competitive conflict for quality supply partnerships between China and Hong Kong. *International Journal of Physical Distribution & Logistics Management*, 29(1), pp. 7–21.

Wong, A.S.H., Tjosvold, D., and Yu, Z.Y., 2005. Organizational partnerships in China: Self-interest, goal interdependence, and opportunism. *Journal of Applied Psychology*, 90(4), pp. 782–91.

Wu, J.L. and Tjosvold, D., 2010. *Goal Interdependence and Managing in Supply Chain Partnerships in China*. Presented at the 23rd Annual Conference of International Association for Conflict Management, Boston, USA.

12   Reflection: Learning to be a Better Team

Argyris, C. and Schon, D., 1978. *Organizational Learning: A Theory of Action Approach*. Reading, MA: Addision Wesley.

Index

Printed and bound by CPI Group (UK) Ltd, Croydon, CR0 4YY